JEFFERSON AT MONTICELLO.

THE PRIVATE LIFE OF

THOMAS JEFFERSON.

From entirely new Materials.

WITH NUMEROUS FAC-SIMILES.

BY

REV. HAMILTON W. PIERSON, D. D.,

PRESIDENT OF CUMBERLAND COLLEGE, KY.

NEW YORK:
CHARLES SCRIBNER, 124 GRAND STREET.
1862.

JOHN F. TROW,
PRINTER, STEREOTYPER, AND ELECTROTYPER,
48 & 50 Greene Street,
New York.

TO

MY OLD COLLEGE CHUM,

REV. SILAS S. HARMON,

OF SONORA, CALIFORNIA.

IN MEMORY OF

THE FOUR DELIGHTFUL YEARS

WHEN

WE STUDIED, WALKED, AND TALKED TOGETHER,

AND

SO OFTEN AND SO TRULY SAID,

HAEC OLIM MEMINISSE JUVABIT,

This Volume

IS

RESPECTFULLY DEDICATED,

AS A TRIBUTE

TO HIS RARE ATTAINMENTS AS A SCHOLAR,

HIS SELF-DENYING TOILS AS A CHRISTIAN,

AND

HIS TRUE NOBILITY AS A MAN,

BY HIS DEVOTED FRIEND,

THE AUTHOR.

PREFACE.

THIS volume has been prepared from entirely new materials, derived from sources hitherto unexplored. It was the author's rare good fortune, some months since, to make the acquaintance of CAPT. EDMUND BACON, a now aged and wealthy citizen of Kentucky, who was for twenty years the chief overseer and business manager of Mr. Jefferson's estate at Monticello. He obtained from him a large mass of letters and other documents in Mr. Jefferson's own handwriting, giving directions as to his farm, grounds, garden, stock of different kinds, and all the various matters connected with his farm at Monticello. He also spent several weeks in writing out, in detail, Capt. Bacon's reminiscences of his venerated employer. This work has been prepared exclusively from the materials thus acquired. It is not therefore a rearrangement of historical facts in regard to Mr Jefferson, that were already known and accessible to the public, but a presentation of those that are entirely new.

It does not come within the scope or design of this work, to attempt any sketch of Mr. Jefferson's public life, or any discussion of his political or religious opinions. Its simple purpose is, so to describe his home, his personal appearance, and all his personal and business habits, as to set the *man* fully before the reader—as a farmer, manufacturer, and master; as a lover of fine horses, hogs, and sheep; as the enthusiastic cultivator of fruits and flowers; as the kind neighbor; the liberal benefactor of the poor; the participator in the childish sports of his grandchildren; the hospitable entertainer of swarms of visitors, that well-nigh ate up his substance and consumed his life; and in all the minutest details of his every-day home life at Monticello. It is believed that the portraiture of Mr. Jefferson's Private Life, thus presented, is much more full and complete than any that has heretofore been given to the public.

There are a few facts in this volume that, if the author could have consulted his own feelings merely, he would certainly have omitted. He has described at length, in the first chapter, the manner in which all Capt. Bacon's reminiscences were obtained and written out. The facts alluded to were secured in the same manner, but afterwards were marked to be omitted from the volume. A distinguished historian who was looking over the manuscript, asked why those passages were to be omitted. The author replied, that he did not like to publish facts that would give pain to any that might now be living.

"Did you ever know," said he, "a kinder-hearted man than the Apostle John? And did he not tell us that Peter denied his Master—more than once! And would not his history have been very imperfect, if he had failed to give us this fact? What is your praise worth, if you suppress all facts that are not praiseworthy?"

The author could but feel the force of these questions, and could not erase the sad facts that are presented in regard to the intemperance, and other vices and misfortunes, of some who were connected with Mr. Jefferson's family, and otherwise make a part of this history. It was the fault of David that he sinned, and not of the sacred historian that he recorded the fact. The principle involved in this judgment, is of universal application.

The author submits this volume to the public with entire confidence in the credibility of the testimony of the venerable man from whom so many of the facts presented have been obtained. At this memorable period of our country's history, when the Union that was established by the wisdom and cemented by the blood of our venerated fathers, has been so madly assailed, he is happy to have been the means of rescuing from oblivion facts that must increase our national reverence and regard for one of the most distinguished founders of our Republic, and administrators of its Government.—Esto Perpetua.

Cumberland College, Princeton, Ky., 1862.

CONTENTS.

CHAPTER I.

INTRODUCTION TO CAPT. BACON.

CHAPTER II.

AUTOBIOGRAPHY OF CAPT. EDMUND BACON.

CHAPTER III.

MONTICELLO.

CHAPTER IV.

MR. JEFFERSON'S BLOODED STOCK.

CHAPTER V.

MR. JEFFERSON'S MANUFACTORIES.

CHAPTER VI.

MR. JEFFERSON'S PERSONAL APPEARANCE AND HABITS.

CHAPTER VII.

MR. JEFFERSON'S FAMILY.

CHAPTER VIII.

MR. JEFFERSON'S SERVANTS.

CHAPTER IX.

MR. JEFFERSON AT WASHINGTON—HIS LIBRARY.

CHAPTER X.

MR. JEFFERSON'S HOSPITALITY.

JEFFERSON AT MONTICELLO.

CHAPTER I.

INTRODUCTION TO CAPT. BACON.

DEATH OF JEFFERSON AND ADAMS—"THOMAS JEFFERSON STILL SURVIVES," IN THE MEMORY OF HIS OVERSEER—VISIT TO HIS NEIGHBOR, CAPT. ROACH—ANECDOTE OF JOHN RANDOLPH—INTRODUCTION TO CAPT. BACON—MR. JEFFERSON AND THE UNIVERSITY OF VIRGINIA—SELECTION OF THE SITE—LAYING OF THE CORNER-STONE—INTEREST IN THE ERECTION OF THE UNIVERSITY—MR. JEFFERSON'S LETTER OF RECOMMENDATION TO CAPT. BACON—CAPT. BACON'S HORSES—HIS KNOWLEDGE OF BLOODED STOCK—JOHN RANDOLPH'S BLOODED HORSES—SUBSEQUENT VISITS TO CAPT. BACON—MANNER OF TAKING NOTES AND PREPARING THIS VOLUME.

"THOMAS JEFFERSON STILL SURVIVES!" were the dying words of the elder Adams. At that moment the devoted family and friends, at Monticello and at Quincy, were moving with the same noiseless tread, and watching with the same breathless interest, the closing scenes in the lives of those illustrious men. Adams and Jefferson breathed their last, July 4th, 1826; and the waves of grief from Quincy and Monticello soon intermingled and overspread the land. The nation was in tears. Adams and Jefferson were no more. The one by his tongue, the other by his pen, had done more than any others, by these means, to secure the liberty and independence of their country. That country had lavished upon each her highest honors; and, as if in approval of their life-work, Heaven had kindly ordained that both should die upon the anniversary of that day that they had done so much to make immortal.

These pages are devoted especially to the memory of Jefferson. The dying utterance of the sage of Quincy was not less the statement of a fact, than a prophecy. Thomas Jefferson still survives. Thomas Jefferson will survive so long as our country or its history endures. That he was the author of the Declaration of Independence; that he filled the highest posts of public trust at home and abroad; that his name and influence are interwoven with the early history of his State and country; that he was the founder of the University of Virginia;—these facts, and such as these, are well known to all. In all these relations, Thomas Jefferson still survives in history and in the universal knowledge of his countrymen.

But it will doubtless be new to most of my readers, that Thomas Jefferson still survives in all the minutest details of his every-day home life at Monticello; as a farmer, manufacturer, and master; as a lover of fine horses, hogs, and sheep; as the enthusiastic cultivator of fruits and flowers; as the kind neighbor, the liberal benefactor of the poor, the participator in the childish sports of his grandchildren, the hospitable entertainer of swarms of visitors that well-nigh ate up all his substance, and consumed his life;—in all these, and numerous other relations, Thomas Jefferson still survives in the iron memory, and in the most devoted and tender affection and veneration of a now aged man, who was for twenty years the chief overseer and business manager of his estate at Monticello. Such is the fact.

On a visit, some months since, with one of my associates, to a neighborhood in Trigg County, Ky., about twenty miles from my own home, our host, Capt. C. W. Roach, remarked: "I have a near neighbor, Capt. Edmund Bacon, who lived with Thomas Jefferson at Monticello, as overseer, for twenty years."

"We should be most happy to go and see him," was our response; and very soon we were on our way. Most naturally, as we rode on, our conversation turned on the distinguished men that Virginia had given to the country and the world. Though I doubt not my readers are as impatient for the introduction that was before us as we were, I am sure they will pardon me for detaining them with some of the details of that conversation.

Capt. Roach was a native of Charlotte County, Va., the home of John Randolph. He had been familiar with his appearance from childhood, had frequently heard him speak, had often seen him driving about the country with four magnificent blooded horses to his carriage, and his servants following him with perhaps a dozen more equally "high-bred" and fiery. He gave us a number of anecdotes illustrating his eccentricities. One of these was so very characteristic of the man, that I must repeat it.

A Baptist clergyman, the Rev. Abner W. Clopton, took charge of some Baptist churches in Charlotte County, and attracted unusual attention as a preacher. He had been a Professor in the University of North Carolina, at Chapel Hill, and the fame of his learning and eloquence drew large crowds to hear him. Mr. Randolph, whose solicitude for his servants is well known, employed Mr. Clopton to preach to them, and generally attended these services. On one occasion, having been particularly moved by the sermon, he arose at its close and commenced an address to his sable audience. As he proceeded, his feelings became deeply enlisted, and in the most appropriate, beautiful, and eloquent manner, he urged upon them the importance of the great moral truths that the preacher had presented to them. Mr. Clopton told Capt. Roach, a few days after, that no clergyman could have spoken more appropriately or beautifully. In conclusion, he expressed his great gratification at seeing them there, said he was very glad to provide preaching for them, was willing and anxious to afford them all the religious privileges they could desire, *except night meetings.* He could not and would not tolerate them. He grew indignant and bitter as he went on to speak of their evil effects, and said there was nothing that he hated worse, unless it was a mean, thieving overseer, to whom, in his indignation, he applied another and much stronger epithet, not at all in keeping with the moral lecture he had just given. As quick as thought he set about extricating himself from the awkward condition into which he had been led by his passions, and very deliberately went on to say, "Now if there were any common, vulgar people here, they would perhaps go away and say that I had used profane language; but my clerical friend here, who is a fine classical scholar, knows that 'damned' means condemned; and therefore I simply mean to say, an overseer that everybody condemns."

As we approached our destination, I remarked

to Capt. Roach, that as it was so late in the afternoon, we should have but a short time to stay, and I was anxious to spend as little time as possible in general conversation, so that we might hear as much as possible of Mr. Jefferson from one who had been with him so many years, and must have known him so well.

"Give yourself no uneasiness about that," said he. "Capt. Bacon is enthusiastic and entirely at home on two subjects, and he never tires of talking about either. One is Thomas Jefferson, and the other is fine horses; and he easily passes from one to the other. We shall not be in the house many minutes before you will be certain to hear something of Mr. Jefferson."

We entered the house, and were introduced to Capt. Bacon as connected with the College at Princeton. The form of our introduction was most fortunate. It was pivotal. To Capt. Bacon's mind the mention of a College most naturally suggested the University of Virginia, and Mr. Jefferson's labors and solicitude in its behalf. He began at once to give the early history of the institution, and we soon found not only that he could talk about Mr. Jefferson, but that he was an uncommonly interesting talker, as the reader shall have occasion to see, for my pencil was soon in requisition.

"You know," said he, "that Mr. Jefferson was the founder of the University of Virginia. Let me see if I can remember all the Commissioners. There were Mr. Jefferson, Mr. Madison, Mr. Monroe, Chapman Johnson, John H. Cocke, and some others. They are all that I now remember. The act of the Legislature, if I mistake not, made it their duty to establish the University within a mile of the Court House at Charlottesville. They advertised for proposals for a site. Three men offered sites,—Nicholas Lewis, John H. Craven, and John M. Perry. The Commissioners had a meeting at Monticello, and then went and looked at all these sites. After they had made this examination, Mr. Jefferson sent me to each of them, to request them to send by me their price, which was to be sealed up."

"Do you remember the different prices?" said I.

"I think I do. Lewis and Craven each asked $17 per acre, and Perry $12. That was a mighty big price in those days. I went to Craven and Lewis first. When I went to Perry, he inquired of me if I knew what price the others had asked. I told him I did, but I did not think it would be right for me to tell him. They had both talked the matter over with me, and told me what they were a-going to ask. But I told Perry that if he asked about $10 or $12 per acre, I thought he would be mighty apt to succeed. They took Perry's forty acres, at $12 per acre. It was a poor old turned-out field, though it was finely situated. Mr. Jefferson wrote the deed himself, and I carried it to Mr. Perry, and he signed it. Afterwards Mr. Jefferson bought a large tract near it from a man named Avery. It had a great deal of fine timber and rock on it, which was used in building the University.

"My next instruction was to get ten able-bodied hands to commence the work. I soon got them, and Mr. Jefferson started from Monticello to lay off the foundation, and see the work commenced. An Irishman named Dinsmore, and I, went along with him. As we passed through Charlottesville, I went to old Davy Isaacs' store, and got a ball of twine, and Dinsmore found some shingles and made some pegs, and we all went on to the old field together. Mr. Jefferson looked over the ground some time, and then stuck down a peg. He stuck the very first peg in that building, and then directed me where to carry the line, and I stuck the second. He carried one end of the line, and I the other, in laying off the foundation of the University. He had a little rule in his pocket that he always carried with him, and with this he measured off the ground, and laid off the entire foundation, and then set the men at work. I have that rule now, and here it is," said Capt. Bacon, taking it from a drawer in his secretary that he unlocked, to show it to us. It was a small twelve-inch rule, so made as to be but three inches long when folded up. "Mr. Jefferson and I were once going along the bank of the canal," said he, "and in crawling through some bushes and vines, it fell out of his pocket and slid down the bank into the river. Some time after that, when the water had fallen, I went and found it, and carried it to Mr. Jefferson. He told me I had had a great deal of trouble to get it, and as he had provided himself with another, I could keep it. I intend to keep it as long as I live; and when I die, that rule can be found locked up in that drawer.

"After the foundation was nearly completed, they had a great time laying the corner-stone. The old field was covered with carriages and people. There was an immense crowd there. Mr. Monroe laid the corner-stone. He was President at that time. He held the instruments, and pronounced it square. He only made a few remarks, and Chapman Johnson and several others made speeches. Mr. Jefferson—poor old man!—I can see his white head just as he stood there and looked on.

"After this he rode there from Monticello every

day while the University was building, unless the weather was very stormy. I don't think he ever missed a day unless the weather was *very* bad. Company never made any difference. When he could not go on account of the weather, he would send me, if there was any thing that he wanted to know. He looked after all the materials, and would not allow any poor materials to go into the building if he could help it. He took as much pains in seeing that every thing was done right, as if it had been his own house."

After answering a great many questions in regard to Mr. Jefferson, Capt. Bacon said he had a great many of his letters, and proposed to show us a specimen of his handwriting. He unlocked a drawer, and brought us a paper, which most naturally he prizes very highly, of which the following is a copy:

"WARM SPRINGS, Aug. 18, 1818.

"The bearer, Mr. Edmund Bacon, has lived with me twelve years as manager of my farm at Monticello. He goes to the Missouri to look out for lands to which he means to remove. He is an honest, correct man in his conduct, and worthy of confidence in his engagements. Any information or instruction which any person may give him, will be worthily bestowed; and if he should apply particularly to Gov. Clarke on his way, the Governor will especially oblige me by imparting to him his information and advice.

"THOMAS JEFFERSON."

"Mr. Bacon has continued to possess the esteem, confidence, and good-will of his neighbors, and of the family in which he has lived, without any interruption to this day.

"TH. M. RANDOLPH."

"*September* 14, 1820."

I will here add, that Capt. Bacon has now resided in Kentucky about forty years, and his neighbors, who have known him during all that time, would vouch as strongly for his character as Mr. Jefferson and his son-in-law, Gov. Randolph, have done. He is a man of wealth and character.

Our time was exhausted, and expressing our great gratification at our visit, we arose to leave; but Capt. Bacon insisted that we should go to his stable and see his horses. He had two of them brought out and exhibited for our gratification. They were magnificent specimens of that noble animal. Their pedigrees for an indefinite period backward were at his tongue's end, and he showed a knowledge of blooded horses that I think would have astonished any old Virginia connoisseur in that line. He was certainly thoroughly Jeffersonian in his love for fine horses. He had taken the leading stock journals of the country for more than fifty years, and seemed to know all about all the most noted horses there had been in the country in all that time. Like Mr. Jefferson, he has never patronized nor in any way encouraged horse-racing. He says, that though John Randolph had sometimes a hundred* blooded horses,—the finest stable of horses in Virginia,—he never trained them for the turf—never allowed them to race.

On leaving, I told Capt. Bacon, that if my life was spared, that would not be my last visit to him. I felt that I had found a rich historical *placer*, that I was determined to thoroughly work, as soon as I could find time to do so.

---

* "CHARLOTTE COUNTY, VA., May 19, 1826.

* * * * * * "Mr. Randolph is the Magnus Apollo of this county. Every one knows and fears him. His power of sarcasm and invective is such, that no one pretends to contradict him. He has three several plantations in this county, all of them extensive. His horses (I mean those which are never used) are worth, I suppose, about $8,000."

"CHARLOTTE, April 10, 1827.

* * * * * * "This part of Virginia has long been celebrated for its breed of horses. There is a scrupulous attention paid to the preservation of the immaculate English blood. Among the crowd on this day were snorting and rearing fourteen or fifteen stallions, some of which were indeed fine specimens of that noble creature. Among the rest, Mr. Randolph's celebrated English horse Roanoke, who is nine years old, and has never been 'backed.'"—*Forty Years' Familiar Letters of James W. Alexander, D.D. New York: Chas. Scribner.* 1860. Pp. 95, 101.

I have recently been able to accomplish that determination. I have spent several weeks with my host, to whom I was indebted for this introduction, and day after day I have gone to Capt. Bacon's, and listened to his reminiscences of his venerated employer. He was never weary of talking on this theme, nor I of listening. At his fireside, around his hospitable table, strolling among his blooded stock, and riding over his immense plantation, he poured forth from the inexhaustible storehouse of his wonderful memory the accumulations of a score of the best years of his life, that were spent at Monticello. It will be my object in the pages that follow, to give the results of these conversations. I shall not trouble the reader with the thousand questions I have asked, but will give the answers in narrative form, as nearly as possible in Capt. Bacon's own language. He has frequently remarked to me, that when he was a boy, there were no such opportunities for education as now; that he had only an "old-field-school, picked-up education;" but the reader will see that he has "picked up" a very terse, vigorous use of language. This is no doubt largely due to the unconscious influence of Mr. Jefferson, for whom his admiration is most profound, and was acquired in his twenty years' correspondence and conversations with him in regard to his business affairs.

In my visits to Capt. Bacon, I took notes of all that he said of Mr. Jefferson. Sometimes he would talk at length upon one subject, and at others his conversation was perfectly discursive. But wherever he went I followed him with my "notes," asking him questions and drawing him out whenever his mind seemed most excited by his own reminiscences upon particular themes. In this manner we talked, and I wrote day after day, until I had gained from him all the information I could possibly acquire in regard to Mr. Jefferson. Having in this manner filled a blank book with "notes," and having carefully looked over Capt. Bacon's papers, and selected, by his permission, all those in the handwriting of Mr. Jefferson, Mr. Monroe, Mr. Randolph, and some others, I returned home with my historical treasures.

In writing this volume, I have done very little "editing," except that the results of these conversations are arranged, as far as possible, under the subjects to which they appropriately belong. The reader will bear in mind, that these reminiscences go back over a period of from forty to sixty years; yet in no instance has Capt. Bacon referred to a manuscript or written memorandum in regard to any of the facts communicated. They are literally "reminiscences." It is therefore well-nigh impossible that there should be no inaccuracies in any of the statements. Should any reader make such a discovery, I am sure that in the circumstances he will need no exhortation from me, in behalf of my aged friend, to

> "Be to his faults a little blind;
> Be to his virtues very kind."

Before proceeding with these reminiscences of Mr. Jefferson, it will be proper for me *more fully* to introduce Capt. Bacon to my readers. This I shall do in the next chapter.

CHAPTER II.

CAPT. BACON'S AUTOBIOGRAPHY.

BIRTH—FAMILY—EARLY ACQUAINTANCE WITH MR. JEFFERSON—EMPLOYED BY HIM AS OVERSEER—WITH HIM TWENTY YEARS—VISIT TO ST. LOUIS IN 1818—THE PARTY—JOURNEY ON HORSEBACK—FORDING RIVERS—DEER, WOLVES, AND WILD GAME ON THE ROUTE—GOV. COLES AND HIS SLAVES AT EDWARDSVILLE, ILL.—ST. LOUIS A SMALL FRENCH SETTLEMENT—GOV. CLARKE—HIS VIEWS OF THE FUTURE OF ST. LOUIS—CHOUTEAU'S FARM—HIS ANXIETY TO SELL—REASONS FOR NOT PURCHASING—RETURN TO MONTICELLO—SUBSEQUENT EMIGRATION TO KENTUCKY—SECOND VISIT TO MISSOURI—THE KENTUCKY WIDOW—DETERMINATION TO RETURN AND MARRY—SATISFIED WITH THE UNION.

"I AM now seventy-six years old. I was born March 28, 1785, within two or three miles of Monticello, so that I recollect Mr. Jefferson as far back as I can remember anybody. My father and he were raised together, and went to school together. My oldest brother, William Bacon, had charge of his estate during the four years he was Minister to France. After he was elected President, he told my father he wanted an overseer, and he wished to employ my brother William again. But he was then quite an old man, and very well off, and did not wish to go. He then inquired of my father if he could not spare me. He replied that he thought I was too young. I was his youngest son, and not of age yet. Mr. Jefferson requested him to send me to see him about it. My father was a comfortable farmer; had ten or twelve hands. He was very industrious, and taught all his children to work. Mr. Jefferson knew this. That was why he wanted one of my father's sons. He was the most industrious man I ever knew. When my father told me Mr. Jefferson wanted to employ me, I was keen to go; and I determined that if he employed me, I would please him, if there was any such thing. When I went to see him, he told me what he wanted me to do, gave me good advice, and said he would try me, and see how I would get along. I went to live with him the 27th of the December before he was inaugurated as President; and if I had remained with him from the 8th of October to the 27th of December, the year that I left him, I should have been with him precisely twenty years.

"Some time before I left him, I determined to go West and buy land upon which to settle, and Mr. Jefferson recommended me to go to the Missouri. It was a territory then, and there was a great deal of talk about it. At the time that we had arranged that I should go and look at the country, Mr. Jefferson was at the Warm Springs.

In going to his Bedford farm, he had somehow caught the itch, and it troubled him a great deal, and he went to the Springs to see if he could not get rid of it. But he wrote me not to let his absence interrupt my plans, and said that in going, I would pass directly through the yard where he was staying, and he would see me there. That is why that letter of his, that I showed you, is dated at the Warm Springs.

"There were six of us started together on horseback from Charlottesville for the Missouri,—John D. Coles, Absalom Johnson, James Garnett, William Bacon, and —— Jones—I forget his given name; he was as good company as ever lived. We went by the Warm Springs, Hot Springs, Guyandotte, and crossed the Big Sandy at its mouth; and then went on by Flemingsburg, Mt. Sterling, Lexington, and Shelbyville, to Louisville. It was a little settlement then, and the people were very anxious we should settle there. When we crossed the Ohio into Indiana, there was no road at all. We took a pilot, and went to Vincennes. We had no road, only a bridle path. From there we went to Edwardswille, Ill., where Edward Coles, afterwards Governor of the State, then lived. I had known him well in Albemarle County; we were raised together. He was very anxious for us to buy land there. He had bought a great deal. He had taken about twenty negroes with him from Virginia, who worked for him for a time, and made improvements on his land. He finally sold his land for a great profit, freed his negroes, and went back to Virginia. From here we went on to St. Louis.

"There were no bridges on our route, and only the large rivers, like the Ohio and Mississippi, had ferry-boats. We had to swim all the smaller streams. Some of the more difficult streams had dug-out canoes, in which we rowed over, and swam our horses behind and beside us. My mare was one of the best animals ever backed. She was a granddaughter of imported Diomede. She would swim almost like a fish. She would seldom wet me above the knees. Garnett's horse was a poor swimmer—swam very deep. He called him Henry. When we crossed a river, you could only see his head out of the water, and Garnett would be wet almost to the armpits. On our way we saw a great deal of game,—gangs of deer, fowls, and wolves. At one house where we stayed all night, the wolves came about the house and howled so terribly, that the dogs were afraid of them—would not go out and attack them. They took several pigs out of the pen, and we had to go out and throw brands of fire at them to drive them away. We saw no bears except some tame ones that had been caught by the people when they were young.

"When we got to St. Louis, I called on Gov. Clarke, and showed him the letter from Mr. Jefferson, and I never was more kindly treated. There was a small tavern near the ferry, but he insisted that I should stay with him. He knew a great deal about the Western country. He and Merriwether Lewis had explored the Missouri River. St. Louis was a dingy little settlement, not much larger than a good negro quarter. There was only one narrow street three or four hundred yards long. The houses were mostly old-looking, built of rock in the roughest manner possible. A few of them were plastered houses. They were all one story. Gov. Clarke lived in a one-story plastered house with two rooms. The fences around their truck patches (gardens) were a kind of wicker-work made of posts stuck into the ground, and brush wattled into them. For miles around it was a prairie country. Back from the river some two or three miles, there was a large spring, and near it a windmill that did most of the grinding for the settlement. I went out there several times. When the wind blew hard, it ground very fast. Most of the people were French. Even the negroes spoke French. Gov. Clarke was very anxious that I should buy there. He advised me to look no further. He said that with so many large rivers coming in near there, and such a rich, fertile country, it must some day be a large place. He told me there was a Frenchman named Chouteau who had a great deal of land there, and was very anxious to sell a thousand acres. He said the Frenchman needed every thing but land. I went to see him, and Clarke sent his clerk along with me to interpret. He was almost as black as a negro, lived in a low, squatty brick house, almost without furniture. It had benches in place of chairs. He was very anxious to sell, and only asked me three dollars an acre for a thousand acres. I concluded to look further over the Territory. We got a pilot, and travelled several hundred miles over the country north and south of the Missouri River, and returned to St. Louis. Chouteau sent to me several times to urge me to buy of him, and Clarke persuaded me to it very strongly. If I had only taken his advice! I had $3,000 in a belt around me; but by this time I had concluded I would not take off my belt and pay out my money for all the land in the Territory. You could raise abundance of every thing, but could get nothing for it. There was no such thing as a steamboat on any Western river. Such a thing wasn't thought of then. Keel and flat-boats were the only kind of navigation. The people told me how they did. When they had a surplus of bacon, flour, and venison, they would load up a flat-boat and take it to New Orleans. It took four or five months to make the trip, and they got very little for their load. It was a solemn sight to see a boat start off. The people would assemble on the bank of the river, and bid their friends farewell. It was very uncertain whether they would ever see them again, for they were going into a dead, sickly place, and they had to walk all the way back through an Indian country.

"I returned to Virginia without making any purchase, remained a few years longer with Mr. Jefferson, and then removed my family to Kentucky, and rented a farm until I could look over the country and satisfy myself. I went to St. Louis and looked over the State again, but could not make up my mind to settle there. Chouteau was still anxious to sell, and Clarke anxious that I should buy; but I concluded that Kentucky was far enough West, and that I would go back and buy there."

Could Capt. Bacon have looked into the future, he would have purchased the thousand acres which are now covered by the city of St. Louis. It is now very easy to see how he missed an immense fortune. "If our foresight was as good as our hindsight, it would be an easy matter to get rich." But Capt. Bacon is not particularly to be pitied in this regard. He purchased, at two dollars per acre, a thousand acres of much better farming land, where he now resides, to which he has since made additions, until he now has about four thousand acres. This, with a large amount of most valuable stock, and (as his neighbors tell me) a good many thousand dollars at interest, make a fortune so ample as to leave very little room for reasonable regret in regard to his decision at St. Louis.

Moreover, there were potent reasons for that decision. Gov. Clarke, in his prophetic portraiture of the brilliant future that was before St. Louis, and in all his other earnest and eloquent persuasives, was opposed by pleadings that he wot not of. He was engaged in an unequal contest.

Capt. Bacon was a widower. His wife had died in Kentucky. Kentucky, so famed as "the dark and bloody ground," is not less famed for the unerring execution of other than Indian archers. Many a passing traveller has received their darts,—has been taken captive. Capt. Bacon had seen a Kentucky widow. He shall tell the rest.

We were sitting around his large old-fashioned fireplace, as was our wont. Mrs. Bacon, who at seventy-six is hale and hearty, and as active as most ladies at thirty or forty, was sitting in one "corner" by her window, busy with her knitting, and absorbed with the conversation. Capt. Bacon was near her, his face all aglow with his own reminiscences of long-gone years, and the writer was in the other corner, with pencil and note-book in hand. With a smile that indicated the most perfect satisfaction with the whole result, Capt. Bacon gave the following "explanation" of his failure to make the St. Louis purchase:

"The fact is, sir," said he, "I believe I should have bought in St. Louis, if it had not been for the old lady here. I had seen her. The last night I was in St. Louis, I determined I would go back and marry her, if possible, and settle here. We have now lived together nearly forty years, and I believe neither of us is tired of the union, or anxious to secede."

CHAPTER III.

MONTICELLO.

THE MOUNTAIN, MANSION, GROUNDS, FLOWERS, SHRUBBERY, TERRACED GARDEN —FRUIT, VEGETABLES—LETTER OF INSTRUCTIONS FROM WASHINGTON IN REGARD TO STOCK, CROPS, ACCOUNTS, SHRUBBERY, ETC.—THE ESTATE—DIFFERENT PLANTATIONS—PREMIUMS TO OVERSEERS AND SERVANTS—COPY OF MR. JEFFERSON'S INSTRUCTIONS ON LEAVING HOME FOR WASHINGTON.

CAPT. BACON says:—"Monticello is quite a high mountain, in the shape of a sugar-loaf. A winding road led up to the mansion. On the very top of the mountain the forest trees were cut down, and ten acres were cleared and levelled off. This was done before I went to live with Mr. Jefferson. The house in the picture that you showed me, (Frontispiece,) is upon the highest point. That picture is perfectly natural. I knew every room in that house. Under the house and the terraces that surrounded it, were his cisterns, ice-house, cellar, kitchen, and rooms for all sorts of purposes. His servants' rooms were on one side. They were very comfortable, warm in the winter and cool in the summer. Then there were rooms for vegetables, fruit, cider, wood, and every other purpose. There were no negro and other out-houses around the mansion, as you generally see on plantations. The grounds around the house were most beautifully ornamented with flowers and shrubbery. There were walks, and borders, and flowers, that I have never seen or heard of anywhere else. Some of them were in bloom from early in the spring until late in the winter. A good many of them were foreign. Back of the house was a beautiful lawn of two or three acres, where his grandchildren used to play a great deal. His garden was on the side of the mountain. I had it built mostly while he was President. It took a great deal of labor. We had to blow out the rock for the walls for the different terraces, and then make the soil. I have some of the instructions that Mr. Jefferson sent me from Washington now. It was a fine garden. There were vegetables of all kinds, grapes, figs, and the greatest variety of fruit. I have never seen such a place for fruit. It was so high that it never failed. Mr. Jefferson sent home a great many kinds of trees and shrubbery from Washington. I used to send a servant there with a great many fine things from Monticello for his table, and he would send back the cart loaded with shrubbery from a nursery near Georgetown, that belonged to a man named Maine, and he would always send me directions what to do with it. He always knew all about every thing in every part of his grounds and garden. He knew the name of every tree, and just where one was dead or missing. Here is a letter that he sent me from Washington:

"'WASHINGTON, Nov. 24, 1807.

"'SIR,—Davy has been detained till now, the earth having been so frozen that the plants could not be dug up. On the next leaf are instructions what to do with them, in addition to which I inclose Mr. Maine's instructions as to the thorns. He brings a couple of Guinea pigs, which I wish you to take great care of, as I propose to get this kind into the place of those we have now, as I greatly prefer their size and form. I think you had better keep them in some inclosure near your house till spring. I hope my sheep are driven up every night, and carefully attended to. The finishing every thing about the mill, is what I wish always to have a preference to every kind of work. Next to that, my heart is most set on finishing the garden. I have promised Mr. Craven that nothing shall run next year in the meadow inclosure, where his clearing will be. This is necessary for ourselves, that we may mow the clover and feed it green. I have hired the same negroes for another year, and am promised them as long as I want them. Stewart must be immediately dismissed. If he will do those jobs I mentioned before he goes, he may stay to do them, and have provisions while about them. Joe may work in the way you proposed, so that the whole concern may be together. I place here the statement of debts and remittances:

DEBTS.

Jacob Cooper,	£8	1s.	6d.	=	$26 92
John Peyton,	21	12	3	=	72 04
Dr. Jamieson,	7	10	0	=	35 00
James Carr, corn,					35 00
Thomas Burras, 18 hogs,					20 75
Richard Anderson, flour,					13 00
John Rogers, beef and corn,					117 00
James Butler, flour,					10 00
Do. beeves,					85 00
Robt. Burras, 20 barrels corn,					35 00
Robt. Terril, 100 do.					175 00
Do. 10,000 lbs. fodder,					50 00
Your own balance,					133 33
					$808 04

REMITTANCES.

Oct. 12.	Remitted,	$101 00
Nov. 9.	Do.	110 00
Dec. 6.	By Mr. Craven,	200 00
	To the order of Kelly,	33 33
Jan.	I shall remit	260 00
Feb.	Do.	103 71
		$808 04

"'By these remittances and payments made and to be made, you will perceive that the whole will be paid off by the first week in February. Mr. Craven called on me the 17th, with your order to pay him $100 the first week in December; but he said you would receive $200 of his money, and that he should be extremely distressed if he could not get the whole sum here. On that I gave him my note to pay $200 to his order the first week of next month, and you are to use his $200 instead of what I intended to remit you at that time. Last night I received from Mr. Kelly your order to pay him $133⅓. To reconcile these two transactions, you can use $100 of Craven's money towards paying the debts. Pay Mr. Kelly $100 of it, in part of your order on me, and I will remit $33⅓, according to his order, by which means every thing will be brought to rights. I shall write to him on this subject, and shall be glad to learn that this arrangement is made, and is satisfactory.

"'I tender you my best wishes.

"'TH. JEFFERSON.'

"'DIRECTIONS FOR MR. BACON.

"'If the weather is not open and soft when Davy arrives, put the box of thorns into the cellar, where they may be entirely free from the influence of cold, until the weather becomes soft, when they must be planted in the places of those dead through the whole of the hedges which inclose the two orchards, so that the old and the new shall be complete, at 6 inches' distance from every plant. If any remain, plant them in the nursery of thorns. There are 2,000. I send Mr. Maine's written instructions about them, which must be followed most minutely. The other trees he brings are to be planted as follows:

"'4 Purple beaches. In the clumps which are in the southwest and northwest angles of the house, (which Wormley knows.) There were 4 of these trees planted last spring, 2 in each clump. They all died, but the places will be known by the remains of the trees, or by the sticks marked No. IV. in the places. I wish these now sent to be planted in the same places.

"'4 Robinias, or red locusts. In the clumps in the N.E. and S.E. angles of the house. There were 2 of these planted last spring, to wit, 1 in each. They are dead, and two of them are to be planted in the same places, which may be found by the remains of the trees, or by sticks marked V. The other 2 may be planted in any vacant places in the S.W. and N.W. angles.

"'4 Prickly ash. In the S.W. angle of the house there was planted one of these trees last spring, and in the N.W. angle 2 others. They are dead. 3 of those now sent are to be planted in their places, which may be found by the remains of the trees, or by sticks marked VII. The fourth may be planted in some vacant space of the S.W. angle.

"'6 Spitzenberg apple trees. Plant them in the S.E. orchard, in any place where apples have been planted and are dead.

"'5 Peach trees. Plant in the S.E. orchard, wherever peach trees have died.

"'500 October peach stones; a box of Peccan nuts. The nursery must be enlarged, and these planted in the new parts, and Mr. Perry must immediately extend the paling so as to include these, and make the whole secure against hares.

"'Some turfs of a particular grass. Wormly must plant them in some safe place of the orchard, where he will know them, and keep other grass from the place.'

"I think," said Capt. Bacon, "there were three hundred acres inclosed in the tract about the house. Mr. Jefferson would never allow a tree to be cut off from this. There were roads and paths winding all around and over it, where the family could ride and walk for pleasure. How often I have seen him walking over these grounds, and his grandchildren following after him as happy as they could be.

"The estate was very large. I did know the exact number of acres, for I have paid the taxes a great many times. There was about ten thousand acres. It extended from the town lots of Charlottesville to beyond Milton, which was five or six miles. It was not a profitable estate; it was too uneven and hard to work. Mr. Madison's plantation was much the most profitable. It was divided into four plantations,—Tuffton, Lego, Shadwell, and Pantops. There was a negro quarter and a white overseer at each of these places. A negro named Jim was overseer of the hands at Monticello.

"We used to get up a strife between the different overseers, to see which would make the largest crops, by giving premiums. The one that delivered the best crop of wheat to the hand, had an extra barrel of flour; the best crop of tobacco, a fine Sunday suit; the best lot of pork, an extra hundred and fifty pounds of bacon. Negro Jim always had the best pork, so that the other overseers said it was no use for them to try any more, as he would get it any way. An overseer's allowance of provisions for a year, was: pork, six hundred pounds; wheat flour, two barrels; corn meal, all they wanted. They had gardens, and raised their own vegetables. The servants also had rewards for good conduct.

"I had written instructions about every thing, so that I always knew exactly what to do. Here are the instructions he gave me when he went to Washington:

"'MEMORANDUMS.

"'The first work to be done, is to finish every thing at the mill; to wit, the dam, the stone still wanting in the south abutment, the digging for the addition to the toll mill, the waste, the dressing off the banks and hollows about the mill-houses, making the banks of the canal secure everywhere. In all these things Mr. Walker will direct what is to be done, and how.

"'The second job is the fence from near Nance's house to the river, the course of which will be shown. Previous to this a change in the road is to be made, which will be shown also.

"'As this fence will completely separate the river field from the other grounds, that field is to be cleaned up; the spots in it still in wood are to be cut down where they are not too steep for culture; a part of the field is to be planted in Quarantine corn, which will be found in a tin canister in my closet. This corn is to be in drills 5 feet apart, and the stalks 18 inches asunder in the drills. The rest of the ground is to be sown in oats, and red clover sowed on the oats. All ploughing is to be done horizontally, in the manner Mr. Randolph does his.

"'180 Cords of coal wood are next to be cut. The wood cut in the river field will make a part, and let the rest be cut in the flat lands on the meadow branch south of the overseer's house, which I intend for a Timothy meadow. Let the wood be all corded, that there may be no deception as to the quantity. A kiln will be wanting to be burnt before Christmas; but the rest of the wood had better lie seasoning till spring, when it will be better to burn it.

"'When these things are done, the levelling of the garden is to be resumed. The hands having already worked at this, they understand the work. John best knows how to finish off the levelling.

"'I have hired all the hands belonging to Mrs. and Miss Dangerfield, for the next year. They are nine in number. Moses the miller is to be sent home when his year is up. With these will work in common, Isaac, Charles, Ben, Shepherd, Abram, Davy, John, and Shoemaker Phill; making a gang of 17 hands. Martin is the miller, and Jerry will drive his wagon.

"'Those who work in the nailery, are Moses, Wormly, Jame Hubbard, Barnaby, Isbel's Davy, Bedford John, Bedford Davy, Phill Hubbard, Bartlet, and Lewis. They are sufficient for 2 fires, five at a fire. I am desirous a single man, a smith, should be hired to work with them, to see that their nails are well made, and to superintend them generally; if such an one can be found for $150 or $200 a year, though I would rather give him a share in the nails made, say one-eighth of the price of all the nails made, deducting the cost of the iron; if such a person can be got, Isbel's Davy may be withdrawn to drive the mule wagon, and Sampson join the laborers. There will then be 9 nailers, besides the manager, so that 10 may still work at 2 fires; the manager to have a log house built, and to have 500 lbs. of pork. The nails are to be sold by Mr. Bacon, and the accounts to be kept by him; and he is to direct at all times what nails are to be made.

"'The toll of the mill is to be put away in the two garners made, which are to have secure locks, and Mr. Bacon is to keep the keys. When they are getting too full, the wagons should carry the grain to the overseer's house, to be carefully stowed away. In general, it will be better to use all the bread corn from the mill from week to week, and only bring away the surplus. Mr. Randolph is hopper-free and toll-free at the mill. Mr. Eppes having leased his plantation and gang, they are to pay toll hereafter.

"'Clothes for the people are to be got from Mr. Higginbotham, of the kind heretofore got. I allow them a best striped blanket every three years. Mr.

Lilly had failed in this; but the last year Mr. Freeman gave blankets to one-third of them. This year 11 blankets must be bought, and given to those most in need, noting to whom they are given. The hirelings, if they had not blankets last year, must have them this year. Mrs. Randolph always chooses the clothing for the house servants; that is to say, for Peter Hemings, Burwell, Edwin, Critta, and Sally. Colored plains are provided for Betty Brown, Betty Hemings, Nance, Ursula, and indeed all the others. The nailers, laborers, and hirelings may have it, if they prefer it to cotton. Wool is given for stockings to those who will have it spun and knit for themselves. Fish is always to be got from Richmond, by writing to Mr. Jefferson, and to be dealt out to the hirelings, laborers, workmen, and house servants of all sorts, as has been usual.

"'600 Lbs. of pork is to be provided for the overseer, 500 lbs. for Mr. Stewart, and 500 lbs. for the superintendent of the nailery, if one is employed; also about 900 lbs. more for the people, so as to give them half a pound a-piece once a week. This will require, in the whole, 2,000 or 2,500 lbs. After seeing what the plantation can furnish, and the 3 hogs at the mill, the residue must be purchased. In the winter, a hogshead of molasses must be provided and brought up, which

Mr. Jefferson will furnish. This will afford to give a gill a-piece to everybody once or twice a week.

"'Joe works with Mr. Stewart; John Hemings and Lewis with Mr. Dinsmore; Burwell paints and takes care of the house. With these the overseer has nothing to do, except to find them. Stewart and Joe do all the plantation work; and when Stewart gets into his idle frolics, it may sometimes be well for Moses or Isbel's Davy to join Joe for necessary work.

"'The servants living on the top of the mountain must have a cart-load of wood delivered at their doors once a week through the winter. The fence inclosing the grounds on the top of the mountain must be well done up. This had better be done before they begin the fence down the mountain. No animal of any kind must ever be loose within that inclosure. Mr. Bacon should not fail to come to the top of the mountain every 2 or 3 days, to see that nothing is going wrong, and that the gates are in order. Davy and Abram may patch up the old garden pales when work is going on from which they can best be spared.

"'The thorn hedges are to be kept clean wed at all times. Mr. Dinsmore is to be furnished with bread grain from the mill. The proportion of corn and wheat is left to his own discretion. He provides his own provisions, and for Mr. Nelson and Barry.

"'There is a spout across the canal near the head, which, if left as at present, will do mischief. I will give verbal directions about it.

"'As soon as the Aspen trees lose their leaves, take up one or two hundred of the young trees, not more than 2 or 3 feet high; tie them in bundles, with the roots well covered with straw. Young Davy being to carry Fanny to Washington, he is to take the little cart, (which must be put into the soundest order,) to take these trees on board. 3 Boxes in my study, marked to go by him and Fanny and her things. She must take corn for their meals, and provisions for themselves to Washington. Fodder they can buy on the road. I leave $6 with you, to give them to pay unavoidable expenses. If he could have 2 mules, without stopping a wagon, it would be better. They are to go as soon as the Aspen leaves fall

"'The nailers are to work on the dam till finished, and then go to their shop. The verbal directions which I gave Mr. Bacon respecting Carroll's farm, will be recollected and observed.

"'ADDITIONAL MEMORANDUMS FOR MR. BACON.

"'When the work at the mill is done, and the fence mended up on the top of the mountain, take as much time with your hands as will fill all the gullies in the field north of the overseer's house, (called Belfield,) with bushes, &c., so that they may be filling up by the time we are ready to clean it up. The scalded places should also be covered with bushes.

"'The orchard below the garden must be entirely cultivated the next year; to wit, a part in Ravenscroft pea, which you will find in a canister in my closet; a part with Irish potatoes, and the rest with cow-pea, of which there is a patch at Mr. Freeman's, to save which, great attention must be paid, as they are the last in the neighborhood.

"'Whiskey is wanted for the house, some for Mr. Dinsmore, and some sometimes for the people. About 30 gallons will last a year. Mr. Merriwether or Mr. Rogers may perhaps each let us have some for nails, or will distil it out of our worst toll wheat.

"'In building the house for the nailer, there should be a partition laying off about 8 feet at one end, to keep his nails and rod in.

"'Get from Mr. Perry and Mr. Dinsmore, an estimate of all the nails we shall want for the house in Bedford; and when you have no orders to execute for others, let the boys be making them, and keep them separate from all others; and when the wagon goes up at Christmas, send what shall then be ready.

"'Mr. Higginbotham has all my transportation to and from Richmond under his care. He settles with the watermen, and pays them. I do not wish to have any accounts with them.

"'These rains have possibly spoiled the fodder you had agreed for. You had better see it, and if injured, look out in time for more.

"'Mr. Dinsmore wants Allen's plank brought up immediately. If you choose it, you can take your half beef now, killing one for that purpose, and sending the other half to the house, or to Mr. Randolph's.'"

CHAPTER IV.

MR. JEFFERSON'S BLOODED STOCK.

IMPORTATIONS OF MERINO SHEEP—THEIR GREAT INCREASE IN THE COUNTRY—BARBARY SHEEP FINE MUTTON, BUT NOT POPULAR—CALCUTTA HOGS, VERY FINE—MR. JEFFERSON'S OBJECT IN THE IMPORTATION OF STOCK—HIS PASSION FOR BLOODED HORSES—DESCRIPTION OF DIOMEDE, BRIMMER, WELLINGTON, TECUMSEH, AND EAGLE—HIS TURN-OUT.

"MR. JEFFERSON was very fond of all kinds of good stock. The first full-blooded Merino sheep in all that country, were imported by Mr. Jefferson for himself and Mr. Madison, while he was President. They were sent by water to Fredericksburg. Mr. Jefferson wrote me to go with Mr. Madison's overseer at Montpellier, Mr. Graves, and get the sheep. He said he knew no better way to divide them, than to draw for the choice; and the one who got the first choice of the bucks, take the second choice of the ewes. When we got to Fredericksburg, we were greatly disappointed. The sheep were little bits of things, and Graves said he would not give his riding-whip for the whole lot. There were six of them—two bucks and four ewes. He had the same instructions in regard to dividing them that I had; so I put my hand into my pocket, and drew out a dollar, and said, 'Head, or tail?' He guessed, and I got the first choice. There was a good deal of difference in the bucks, and not much in the ewes. I got the best buck. He was a little fellow, but his wool was as fine almost as cotton. When I got home, I put a notice in the paper at Charlottesville, that persons who wished to improve their stock could send us two ewes, and we would keep them until the lambs were old enough to wean, and then give the owners the choice of the lambs, and they leave the other lamb and both of the ewes. We got the greatest lot of sheep—more than we wanted; two or three hundred, I think; and in a few years we had an immense flock. People came long distances to buy our full-blooded sheep. At first we sold them for fifty dollars, but they soon fell to thirty, and twenty; and before I left Mr. Jefferson, Merino sheep were so numerous, that they sold about as cheap as common ones.

"Some years afterwards he imported, from Barbary, I think, four large broad-tailed sheep. I have forgotten their names. He sent these from Washington in his own wagon, which had gone there with a load from Monticello. These sheep made very fine mutton, but they were not popular—did not disseminate, and ran out in a few years. About the time the first sheep were imported, Mr. Jefferson imported six hogs,—a pair for himself, Mr. Madison, and General Dearborn, one of his secretaries. He often visited Mr. Jefferson. He was a large, fine-looking man. I remember his coming to my house once with Mr. Jefferson, to look at my bees. I had a very large stand; more than forty hives. Those imported hogs were the finest hogs I have ever known. They were called Calcutta hogs. They were black on the heads and rumps, and white-listed round the body. They were very long-bodied, with short legs; were easily kept; would live on grazing, and would scarcely ever root. They would not root much more than an ox. With common pasturage, they would weigh two hundred at a year old; and fed with corn, and well treated, they would weigh three or four hundred.

"Mr. Jefferson didn't care about making money from his imported stock. His great object was to get it widely scattered over the country, and he left all these arrangements to me. I told the people to bring three sows, and when they came for them, they might take two and leave one. In this way he soon got a large number of hogs, and the stock was scattered over that whole country. He never imported any cattle while I was with him.

We could always get remarkably fine cattle from Western Virginia.

"But the horse was Mr. Jefferson's favorite. He was passionately fond of a good horse. We generally worked mules on the plantation; but he would not ride or drive any thing but a high-bred horse. Bay was his preference for color. He would not have any other. After he came from Washington he had a fine carriage built at Monticello, from a model that he planned himself. The wood-work, blacksmithing, and painting, were all done by his own workmen. He had the plating done in Richmond. When he travelled in this carriage, he always had five horses—four in the carriage, and the fifth for Burwell, who always rode behind him. Those five horses were Diomede, Brimmer, Tecumseh, Wellington, and Eagle.

"*Diomede* was a colt of imported Diomede. John W. Eppes, who married Mr. Jefferson's second daughter, Maria, bought Diomede for him in Chesterfield County; gave £80 for him. Eppes wrote Mr. Jefferson that he had bought him, and Mr. Jefferson wrote me to send for him. When I got him home, he was poor, but I had him in fine order when Mr. Jefferson got home. He was a fine high-formed bay horse, not as good for riding as the others, but a fine harness horse. He became blind, poor fellow.

"*Brimmer* was a son of imported Knowlsby. He was a bay, but a shade darker than any of the others. He was a horse of fair size, full, but not quite as tall as Eagle. He was a good riding horse, and excellent for the harness. Mr. Jefferson broke all his horses to both ride and work. I bought Brimmer of General John H. Cocke, of Fluvana County; don't remember what I gave for him. General Cocke was often at Monticello. He used to ride a fine bay stallion called Roebuck, that he had rode in the war of 1812. Sometimes, when he visited Monticello, he would send him to my house, because he had rather trust him with me than with the servants.

"*Tecumseh.* I bought him of old Davy Isaacs, a Jew, who kept a store in Charlottesville. Mr. Jefferson saw him in the field several times as he was riding past, and he told me he was very much pleased with him, and he wished I would make some inquiries about him. I told him that I knew the horse and his stock well. He sent me to buy him. He was a fine horse, but tricky. He would scare at a rock, or when a bird flew up, and jump suddenly. Mr. Jefferson got a blind made that he could attach to his bridle when he rode or drove him, and in this way pretty much cured him.

"*Wellington.* I bought him out of an Augusta County wagon, of a man named Imboden, a Dutchman. Gave £60 for him. He did not know his value. He was a large bay horse, and matched Diomede. He rode better than Diomede, but not as well as the other two.

"*Eagle.* The last thing I ever did for poor old Mr. Jefferson, was to buy Eagle for him for a riding-horse. The last time he ever rode on horseback, he rode Eagle; and the last letter I ever got from Mr. Jefferson, he described that ride, and how Eagle fell with him in the river, and lamed his wrist. I am very sorry I have lost that letter. I bought Eagle of Capt. John Graves, of Louisa County. He was a bay, with white hind ankles, and a white spot on his nose; full sixteen hands high, and the finest sort of a riding-horse.

"In his new carriage, with fine harness, those four horses made a splendid appearance. He never trusted a driver with lines. Two servants rode on horseback, and each guided his own pair. About once a year Mr. Jefferson used to go in his carriage to Montpellier, and spend several days with Mr. Madison; and every summer he went to Poplar Forest, his farm in Bedford, and spent two or three months.

"Mr. Jefferson always knew all about all his stock, as well as every thing else at Monticello, and gave special directions about it all. Here is one of his letters:

"'The sorrel riding-horse is to be kept for Mr. Bacon's riding. If Arcturus has not been exchanged for Mr. Smithson's mare, I wish him and the Chickasaw mare to be disposed of immediately. I think $150 might be expected for him, and $100 for her; but I would take a fair wagon horse or mule for either, rather than keep them. For Arcturus we ought certainly to get a first-rate wagon horse or mule. I would prefer a mule to a horse in both cases, provided they were large and docile.

"'Jerry and his wagon are to go to Bedford before Christmas, and to stay there till they have done all the hauling for my house there. He is to start on the morning of Saturday, the 20th of December, and take with him a bull calf from Mr. Randolph, and the young ram which we have saved for that purpose. He is to proceed to my brother's the first day, and stay there the Sunday. He will take in there some things lodged there last year; to wit, a pair of fowls, some clover seed, and some cow-peas, and proceed with them to Poplar Forest. I promised the friends of the nailers who came from Bedford, to let the boys go and see them this winter; to wit, Jame Hubbard, Phill Hubbard, Bedford John, and Davy. They are to go with the wagon, and assist in conducting the bull and ram. They are to be at home the evening of New Year's day.

"'In all cases of doubt, ask the advice and direction of Mr. Randolph, who will be kind enough to give it.

"'If any beeves remain after I am gone, drive them to Mr. Randolph's, for his use. I should like to have 3 or 4 good milch cows bought, now giving full milk, for the use of the overseer, and people of every description. They should be such as would make good beeves next autumn.

"'Wormley must cover the fig bushes with straw rope. TH. JEFFERSON.'

"'*Sept.* 29, '06.'"

CHAPTER V.

MR. JEFFERSON'S MANUFACTORIES.

FLOURING MILL, VERY EXPENSIVE, AND A BAD INVESTMENT—MR. JEFFERSON'S INTEREST IN IT—LETTERS FROM WASHINGTON—SALE OF FLOUR IN RICHMOND—UNITED STATES BANK MONEY—NAILERY, VERY PROFITABLE—CLOTH FACTORY, BLACKSMITH, CARPENTER, PAINTER.

"MR. JEFFERSON'S neighbors were very anxious that he should build a flouring mill. There was a small one there, but a large one was very much needed. While he was President, they thought he had a large salary, and that he was better able to build one than anybody else. He was always anxious to benefit the community as much as possible, and he undertook it. It cost a great deal of money, and was a very bad investment. I had the foundation dug, and superintended its erection. I have had quantities of letters from him, giving instructions about that mill. He employed a man named Shoemaker, from the North, who was used to building mills, to assist him in planning and building it. It was built of rock. It was a large building, four stories high, and had four run of stone. The dam was three-fourths of a mile above the mill, and a canal was made that distance along the bank of the river, to bring the water to the mill. That dam and canal cost thousands of dollars. Two-thirds of the way, the canal was through blue mountain rock—not limestone—that had to be blown out. It had to be nine feet wide, to allow the bateaux to pass through to Charlottesville. It all cost a great deal of money. After the mill was completed, and we had commenced making flour, there came a big freshet, and swept away the dam. I never felt worse. We had eleven thousand bushels of grain in the mill, and coopers and other hands employed, and I thought we were ruined. But it didn't move him a bit. He never seemed to get tired of paying out money for it. He was always greatly interested in its erection, and in carrying it on. All my letters were full of instructions about it. Here are some of them:

"'MEMORANDUMS FOR MR. BACON.

"'Do the abutment of the dam as soon as the scow is ready, and get the scow made immediately. Then deliver the scow, with a good strong chain of sufficient length, to Mr. Shoemaker.

"'Stop the leak under the bridge just above the waste.

"'Fill up the stone wanting at the waste.

"'Strengthen the bank of the canal at the toll mill.

"'Make the wagon way on the south side of the great mill.

"'Dig the foundation of the wall in the ground floor of the great mill, whenever Mr. Maddox is ready to do the wall, and level the floor.

"'Keep the thorns constantly clean wed.

"'In harvest time send all your hands to assist Mr. Randolph, and let them be with him through his whole harvest, except when wanting to secure our own oats.

"'Wormly must be directed to weed the flower beds about the house, the nursery, the vineyards, and raspberry beds, when they want it.

"'I wish him also to gather me a peck or two of clean broom seed, when ripe.

"'I have bought 3 mules of Mr. Peter Minor in Louisa, which we are to bring home immediately. They are to be broke immediately, but should not be worked more than half their time.

"'Put the Jenny and our 2 mares to the Jack.

"'Give wool to any of my negro women who desire it, as well those with Mr. Craven as others, but particularly to the house women here.

"'I think you should scarcely miss a day visiting the mill, and the top of the mountain also, to see that every thing is right at both places, and particularly that no animals of any kind get into the inclosure at the mountain, or are turned at large into it.

"'Pay great attention to the hogs and sheep. We must get into such a stock as to have 30 killable hogs every year, and fifty ewes. Col. Coles is to have a ram lamb from us of this year. Let it be the best. He will send for it when weaned.

"'Use great economy in timber, never cutting down a tree for fire-wood or any other purpose as long as one can be found ready cut down, and tolerably convenient. In our new way of fencing, the shortest cuts and large branches, and even hollow trees, will come in for use. The loppings will do for fire-wood and coal wood.

"'If a couple more of good mules, two, or rather three years old, can be got for fifty or sixty dollars, at a credit of not less than 90 days from the time I am informed of it, I shall be glad to have them bought. I am told very fine may be got, and cheap, in Fluvana, and particularly that a Mr. Quarles has some to sell.

"'*May* 13, 1807.'

"'WASHINGTON, Nov. 9, 1807.

"'SIR,—

"'I now inclose you $250, of which $100 is for James Walker, $50 for Mr. Maddox, and $100 towards paying such of your debts as are most pressing. Another like remittance the next month will, I hope, begin to place you at your ease. Mr. Peyton sent me an order from Maddox for $50, but at the date of the order you had in hand that sum for him. It will therefore be necessary for you to get Mr. Maddox and Mr. Peyton to agree to which of them this $50 is to be paid. If they do not agree, then it must be paid to Mr. Maddox, as I have not made myself liable for it to Mr. Peyton. I shall be perfectly willing that the waterman to whom you are disposed to sell property should bring up articles for me. I am just now sending off to Richmond 8 trunks of books and 4 other packages, weighing in all about 5,000 weight, as I guess, which will probably be in Richmond in all the last week of this month. They are well secured, but would still require to be as well guarded as possible against rain from above or the water of the boat below. If your boatman will undertake to have special care of them, they will be a good beginning in your account. I tender my best wishes.

" 'TH. JEFFERSON.

" 'MR. E. BACON.'

" 'DIRECTIONS FOR MR. BACON.

" 'June 7, 1808.

" 'Consider as your first object the keeping a full supply of water to the mill, observing that whenever the water does not run over the waste, you should take your hands, and having put in a sufficiency of stone, then carry in earth and heighten till the water runs steadily over the waste. It ought to do this when both mills are running one pair of stones each. Take Mr. Randolph's advice on these occasions.

"'You will furnish Mr. Maddox, while working on the stable, with attendance, hauling, lime, and sand, so that I may only have to pay him for laying the stone. I presume Mr. Dinsmore will let him be of his mess while here. If objected to, however, do for him what you can best.

"'As soon as the sashes are ready for Bedford, furnish Mr. Randolph 3 of your best hands, instead of his waterman, who are to carry the sashes, tables, and other things up to Lynchburg, and to give notice of their arrival to Mr. Chisolm, who will then be in Bedford, and will have Jerry's wagon there, which he must send for the things to Lynchburg. In the mean time, they must be lodged at Mr. Brown's, at Lynchburg.

"'Jerry is to go to Bedford with his wagon as soon as Mr. Chisolm goes.

"'At harvest, give your whole force to Mr. Randolph, to assist in his harvest; the nailers, as well as all the rest, except Johnny Hemings and Lewis.

"'Consider the garden as your main business, and push it with all your might when the interruptions permit.

"'Rake and sweep the charcoal on the level into little heaps, and carry them off. Rather do this when the grass seed is ripe.'

"I used to sell a good deal of the flour in Richmond. The mill was on the Fluvana, the north prong of the James River, and I used to send it down on bateaux. I remember sending off at one time three bateau loads—between two hundred and fifty and three hundred barrels—made of new wheat. I started on horseback in time to get to Richmond before the flour. When I told the landlord I had new flour on the way, 'Well, sir,' said he, 'you will be certain to get a good price for it, for there is hardly a barrel in the city.' I had notice circulated that a lot of new flour would arrive, and be sold at the river at four o'clock. There was a large crowd, and I sold every barrel, at fourteen dollars a barrel, as fast as it could be rolled ashore, and it didn't begin to supply the demand. I got my money from the bank, and started after supper, and rode home that night. It was just sixty-three miles; but I had a fine sorrel mare that Mr. Jefferson appropriated for my use, and I made it easily. As soon as I got home, I went directly to Mr. Jefferson's room with the money. I remember it distinctly. It was the first money of the old United States Bank I had ever seen. The bills were new out of the bank, and very pretty. Mr. Jefferson, you know, was always very strongly opposed to the United States Bank. As I paid it over to him, I remarked that it was very handsome money. 'Yes, sir,' said he, 'and very convenient, if people would only use it properly. But they will not. It will lead to speculation, inflation, and trouble.'

"Mr. Jefferson had a nail factory a good many years, which was a great convenience to the people, and very profitable. He worked ten hands in it—had two fires, and five hands at a fire. These hands could clear two dollars a day, besides paying for the coal and iron rods. After the embargo and the war of 1812, we could not get rods, and were obliged to give it up. We supplied the stores all over that country with nails, and sold a great many to the people to build their houses. I sold Mr. Monroe the nails to build his house.

"Mr. Jefferson also had a factory for making domestic cloth. He got his cotton from Richmond in bateaux. He had in his factory three spinning machines. One had thirty-six spindles, one eighteen, and one six. The hands used to learn on the little one. He made cloth for all his servants, and a great deal besides. I have sold wagon loads of it to the merchants.

"He had a good blacksmith shop. A man named Stewart was at the head of that. He was a fine workman, but he would have his sprees—would get drunk. Mr. Jefferson kept him a good many years longer than he would have done, because he wanted him to teach some of his own hands.

"Dinsmore, who lived with him a good many years, was the most ingenious hand to work with wood I ever knew. He could make any thing. He made a great deal of nice mahogany furniture, helped make the carriage, worked on the University, and could do any kind of fine work that was wanted. Burwell was a fine painter. With all these he could have almost any thing that he needed made on his own plantation."

CHAPTER VI.

MR. JEFFERSON'S PERSONAL APPEARANCE AND HABITS.

MR. JEFFERSON'S HEIGHT—"STRAIGHT AS A GUN-BARREL"—HEALTH, STRENGTH, COMPLEXION, SELF-POSSESSION—ANECDOTE—PERSONAL HABITS—EARLY RISING—HIS FIRE—TOBACCO—CARDS—DIET—INGENUITY—EXERCISE—ATTENDANCE ON PREACHING—ANECDOTE—THE BAPTIST PREACHER—KINDNESS TO THE POOR—FROST OF 1816—ANECDOTE—THE OLD WOMAN AND THE MULE DOLPHIN—BUSINESS HABITS—A WRITTEN ACCOUNT OF EVERY THING—CROP ACCOUNT—CONTRACT FOR WOOD—CONTRACT WITH CARPENTER—WRITTEN CONTRACTS PREVENTED DIFFICULTIES.

"MR. JEFFERSON was six feet two and a half inches high, well proportioned, and straight as a gun-barrel. He was like a fine horse—he had no surplus flesh. He had an iron constitution, and was very strong. He had a machine for measuring strength. There were very few men that I have seen try it, that were as strong in the arms as his son-in-law, Col. Thomas Mann Randolph; but Mr. Jefferson was stronger than he. He always enjoyed the best of health. I don't think he was ever really sick, until his last sickness. His skin was very clear and pure—just like he was in principle. He had blue eyes. His countenance was always mild and pleasant. You never saw it ruffled. No odds what happened, it always maintained the same expression. When I was sometimes very much fretted and disturbed, his countenance was perfectly unmoved. I remember one case in particular. We had about eleven thousand bushels of wheat in the mill, and coopers and every thing else employed. There was a big freshet—the first after the dam was finished. It was raining powerfully. I got up early in the morning, and went up to the dam. While I stood there, it began to break, and I stood and saw the freshet sweep it all away. I never felt worse. I did not know what we should do. I went up to see Mr. Jefferson. He had just come from breakfast. 'Well, sir,' said he, 'have you heard from the river?' I said, 'Yes, sir; I have just come from there with very bad news. The milldam is all swept away.' 'Well, sir,' said he, just as calm and quiet as though nothing had happened, 'we can't make a new dam this summer, but we will get Lewis' ferry-boat, with our own, and get the hands from all the quarters, and boat in rock enough in place of the dam, to answer for the present and next summer. I will send to Baltimore and get ship-bolts, and we will make a dam that the freshet can't wash away.' He then went on and explained to me in detail just how he would have the dam built. We repaired the dam as he suggested, and the next summer we made a new dam, that I reckon must be there yet.

"Mr. Jefferson was always an early riser—arose at daybreak, or before. The sun never found him in bed. I used sometimes to think, when I went up there *very* early in the morning, that I would find him in bed; but there he would be before me, walking on the terrace.

"He never had a servant make a fire in his room in the morning, or at any other time, when he was at home. He always had a box filled with nice dry wood in his room, and when he wanted fire he would open it and put on the wood. He would always have a good many ashes in his fireplace, and when he went out he would cover up his fire very carefully, and when he came back he would uncover the coals and make on a fire for himself.

"He did not use tobacco in any form. He never used a profane word or any thing like it. He never played cards. I never saw a card in the house at Monticello, and I had particular orders from him to suppress card-playing among the negroes, who, you know, are generally very fond of it. I never saw any dancing in his house, and if there had been any there during the twenty years I was with him I should certainly have known it. He was never a great eater, but what he did eat he wanted to be very choice. He never eat much hog-meat. He often told me, as I was giving out meat for the servants, that what I gave one of them for a week would be more than he would use in six months. When he was coming home from Washington I generally knew it, and got ready for him, and waited at the house to give him the keys. After saying, "How are all?" and talking awhile, he would say, "What have you got that is good?" I knew mighty well what suited him. He was especially fond of Guinea fowls; and for meat he preferred good beef, mutton, and lambs. Those broad-tailed sheep I told you about made the finest mutton I ever saw. Merriweather Lewis' mother made very nice hams, and every year I used to get a few from her for his special use. He was very fond of vegetables and fruit, and raised every variety of them. He was very ingenious. He invented a plough that was considered a great improvement on any that had ever been used. He got a great many premiums and medals for it. He planned his own carriage, buildings, garden, fences, and a good many other things. He was nearly always busy upon some plan or model.

"Every day, just as regularly as the day came, unless the weather was very bad, he would have his horse brought out and take his ride. The boy who took care of his horse knew what time he started, and would bring him out for him, and hitch him in his place. He generally started about nine o'clock. He was an uncommonly fine rider—sat easily upon his horse, and always had him in the most perfect control. After he returned from Washington he generally rode Brimmer or Tecumseh until I bought Eagle for him of Capt. John Graves, of Louisa Co., just before I left him.

"He was always very neat in his dress, wore short breeches and bright shoe buckles. When he rode on horseback he had a pair of overalls that he always put on.

"Mr. Jefferson never debarred himself from hearing any preacher that came along. There was a Mr. Hiter, a Baptist preacher, that used to preach occasionally at the Charlottesville Court House. He had no regular church, but was a kind of missionary—rode all over the country and preached. He wasn't much of a preacher, was uneducated, but he was a good man. Everybody had confidence in him, and they went to hear him on that account. Mr. Jefferson's nephews Peter Carr, Sam. Carr, and Dabney Carr thought a great deal of him. I have often heard them talk about him. Mr. Jefferson nearly always went to hear him when he came around. I remember his being there one day in particular. His servant came with him and brought a seat—a kind of camp stool, upon which he sat. After Mr. Jefferson got old and feeble, a servant used to go with him over the plantation, and carry that stool, so that he could sit down while he was waiting and attending to any kind of work that was going on. After the sermon there was a proposition to pass round the hat and raise money to buy the preacher a horse. Mr. Jefferson did not wait for the hat. I saw him unbutton his overalls, and get his hand into his pocket, and take out a handful of silver, I don't know how much. He then walked across the Court House to Mr. Hiter, and gave it into his hand. He bowed very politely to Mr. Jefferson, and seemed to be very much pleased.

"Mr. Jefferson was very liberal and kind to the poor. When he would come from Washington, the poor people all about the country would find it out immediately, and would come in crowds to Monticello to beg him. He would give them notes to me, directing me what to give them. I knew them all a great deal better than he did. Many of them I knew were not worthy—were just lazy, good-for-nothing people, and I would not give them any thing. When I saw Mr. Jefferson I told him who they were, and that he ought not to encourage them in their laziness. He told me that when they came to him and told him their pitiful tales, he could not refuse them, and he did not know what to do. I told him to send them to me. He did so, but they never would come. They knew what to expect.

"In, I think, the year 1816, there was a very severe frost, and the corn was almost destroyed. It was so badly injured that it would hardly make bread, and it was thought that the stock was injured by eating it. There was a neighborhood at the base of the Blue Ridge where the frost did not injure the corn. They had a good crop, and the people were obliged to give them just what they were disposed to ask for it. I went up there and bought thirty barrels for Mr. Jefferson of a Mr. Massey—gave him ten dollars a barrel for it. That spring the poor trifling people came in crowds for corn. I sent the wagon after what I had bought, and by the time it would get back, Mr. Jefferson had given out so many of his little orders that it would pretty much take the load. I could hardly get it hauled as fast as he would give it away. I went to Mr. Jefferson and told him it never would do; we could not give ten dollars a barrel for corn, and haul it thirty miles, and give it away after that fashion. He said, What can I do? These people tell me they have no corn, and it will not do to let them suffer. I told him again, I could tell him what to do. Just send them all to me. I knew them all a great deal better than he did, and would give to all that were really deserving.

"There was an old woman named * * * * who used to trouble us a great deal. She had three daughters that were bad girls—large, strapping, lazy things—and the old woman would beg for them. One day she went to Mr. Jefferson in a mean old dress, and told him some pitiful story, and he gave her a note to me directing me to give her two bushels of meal. I did so. The same day she went to Mrs. Randolph and got three sides of bacon—middling meat. There was more than she could carry, and she had two of her daughters' illegitimate children to help her carry it home. When she got to the river, the old negro who attended the ferry was so mad to see her carrying off the meat that he would not ferry her over. So she laid the meat on the edge of the boat, and they ferried themselves across. When the boat struck the bank it jarred the meat off, and it went to the bottom of the river, and she had a great deal of trouble to get it.

"Afterwards she went to Mr. Jefferson and told him the meal I gave her was not good—would not make bread, and he sent her to me again. I told her the meal in the mill was all alike, and she could only get better by going to the Blue Ridge for the corn. She said she had no horse, it was too far to walk, and she could not go. I told her I would furnish her a mule. Mr. Jefferson had an old mule that must have been thirty or forty years old, called Dolphin. He was too old to work and we did not like to kill him. His hair grew very long, and he was a sight to look at. He was too old to jump much, but he would tear down the fence with his nose and go over the plantation pretty much as he pleased. I was very anxious to get rid of the mule and of the old woman too, and I thought that may be if I loaned her the mule she would not come back. So I told her she could have the old mule and go and get her corn. She came and stayed over night, so as to get an early start. My wife gave her a coffee sack, and I gave her an order on Massey, and she started off on old Dolphin. When she got up there the people knew nothing about her, and she could do so much better begging, that, sure enough, she never came back at all. Mr. Jefferson used to enjoy telling people how I got rid of the old woman and Dolphin. She soon sent for her daughters. Two of them went up there; but a man named * * * * had taken up with one of them, and he moved her off into another neighborhood. He was a well-educated man, and much of a gentleman. His poor old mother was a mighty good woman, and she was so distressed about it that it almost made her crazy.

"Some six weeks or two months after the old woman had gone, I saw something moving about in the wheat-field, and, sure enough, there was Dolphin home again. After this there was a couple of Kentucky drovers named Scott and Dudley, from whom we used to buy a good many mules for the plantation, came along with a drove. I told them about the trouble we had with Dolphin. They said they would take him away so that he would trouble us no more, and I gave him to them. They sheared off his long hair and trimmed him up so that he looked quite well. They found one in the drove that matched him very well, and went on a few miles, and sold the pair to Hon. Hugh Nelson. He was a Congressman. He and Wm. C. Rives married sisters, daughters of Frank Walker. He was very wealthy and popular. I knew his father, too, Col. Walker. He used to wear short breeches and shoe-buckles. It wasn't long before Dolphin was back, and I told Mr. Jefferson. He laughed and said, 'You treat him so much better than anybody else will, that he will come back and see you.' When Mr. Nelson's overseer came over for him I asked him how old he supposed he was. He said he could not tell. I then told him his history. He took him off, and we never saw any more of Dolphin.

"Mr. Jefferson was very particular in the transaction of all his business. He kept an account of every thing. Nothing was too small for him to keep an account of. He knew exactly how much of every thing was raised at each plantation, and what became of it; how much was sold, and how much fed out. Here is one of his little crop accounts. All the overseers had such. Some of them used to grumble over them mightily. But I told them we were paid by Mr. Jefferson to attend to his business, and we ought to do it exactly as he wanted it done. One of them to whom I gave one of these little papers one day, after fretting a good deal about it, said, 'Well, I believe if Mr. Jefferson told you to go into the fire, you would follow his instructions.'

ESTIMATE OF GRAIN.

From Oct. 1, 1819, *to July* 7, 1820, 40 *weeks.*

	Bar.
90 persons from Oct. 1 to July 7.20, 40 weeks, @ 4½ b. a week,	180
70 hogs to be fattened, @ 1½ bar. a piece,	105
9 breeding sows @ 1 pint a day, from Dec. 1 to Mar. 10, 100 days,	3
60 shoats @ ½ pint a day, 100 days,	9½
pigs	5
6 beeves @ 2 gal. a day, from Dec. 1 to Mar. 1 (killing off) say 90 days,	27
Stable @ 14 gals. a day, Oct. 1 to July 1 (deducting 2 mo.) 210 days,	73½
1 plantation horse and 6 mules, @ 1½ bush. a day, Oct. 1 to July 1, 270 d.,	81
Sheep, suppose 80, @ ½ pint from Dec. 1 to Mar. 15, 90 d.,	11
4 oxen @ 6 galls. a day, Dec. 1 to May 15, 165 d.,	25
1 milch cow at the stable, @ 1 peck a day, 165 d.,	8
The other cattle to be fed on stalks, tops, husks, chaff, straw, &c.	
	528

Estimate of grain from Oct. 1. 19 – to July 7. 20 40 weeks

	Bar.
90. persons from Oct. 1. to July 7. 20. – 40. weeks @ 4 1/2 B. a week,	180
70. hogs to be fattened @ 1 1/2 Bar. apiece – – – –	105
9. breeding sows @ 1. pint a day from Dec. 1. to Mar. 10. 100. days	3
60. shoats @ 1/2 pint a day – – – – – – – – 100.	9 1/2
pigs – – – – – – – – – – – – – –	5.
6. beeves @ 2. gal. a day from Dec. 1. to Mar. 1. [killing off] say 90. days	27.
stable @ 14. gal. a day Oct. 1. to July 1. [deducting 2. mo.] 210. days	73 1/2
1. plantation horse & 6. mules @ 1 1/2 bush. a day. Oct. 1. to July 1. 270. d	81
sheep suppose 80 @ 1/2 pint from Dec. 1. to Mar. 15. – – 90. d	11
4. oxen @ 6. gall. a day Dec. 1. to May 15. – – – – 165. d	25
1. milch cow at the stable @ 1 peck a day – – – 165. d	8
the other cattle to be fed on stalks, tops, shucks, chaff, straw &c.	528

Resources

		Bar
Oct. 1. corn on hand in the mill –		80
from Th. J. R. – –		200
mill @ 2. Bar. a week 40. weeks		80
offal of 350. B. flour @ 25 B	35.	
do. to be bought at mill	65	100
		460
340. to be bought elsewhere		68
		528

LITH. OF SARONY, MAJOR & KNAPP. 449 BROADWAY. N.Y.

RESOURCES.

	lb.	b.	Bar.
Oct. 1, corn on hand in the mill,			80
from Th. J. R.			200
Mill @ 2 bar. a week, 40 weeks,			80
Offal of 350 b. flour, @	25	35	
Do. to be bought at mill,		65	100
			460
340 lbs. to be bought elsewhere,			68
			528

"I reported to Mr. Jefferson every dollar that I received and just what I paid it out for. The first day of every January I gave him a full list of all the servants, stock, and every thing on the place, so that he could see exactly what had been the gain or loss. In all his business transactions with people, he had every thing put down in writing, so that there was no chance for any misunderstanding. There was quite a village at Milton. It was the head of navigation for bateaux. A great deal of flour, grain, and other produce was brought from the western part of the State and shipped there, the wagons carrying back groceries and other things that the bateaux had brought from Richmond. This and other business employed a good many families. Nearly all the families in Milton were supplied with firewood from Mr. Jefferson's estate. They paid him five dollars a year for what wood they would burn in a fireplace.

Mr. Jefferson wrote a blank form for me, and I made a written contract with all the people who got their firewood from his place, and once a year I went around and made collections. Here is the blank form that he wrote for me that I filled out, and from which I copied all these contracts for wood:

"'These presents witness that the subscriber, Thomas Jefferson, has leased to the subscriber, James Marr, of the town of Milton, a right, in common with other lessees, to cut and take away sufficient firewood for one fireplace from the lands of the said Thomas Jefferson, on the south side of the road leading through from Milton towards Colle, for the year which began on the 1st day of October last past, and ending the 1st day of October of the present year, 1813; the said James Marr yielding and paying to the said Thomas Jefferson five dollars on the 1st day of October closing the year, which he covenants to do, and it is further agreed that this lease, and on the same conditions, shall continue from year to year until notice to the contrary be given by either party to the other. Witness their hands this 6th day of February, 1813.

TH. JEFFERSON.
"'Witness, JAMES MARR.
"'E. BACON.'

These presents Witness that the subscriber Thomas Jefferson has leased to the subscriber James Marr. —— of the town of Milton, a right in common with other lessees, to cut & take away sufficient firewood for one —— fireplaces from the lands of the sd Thomas Jefferson on the South side of the road leading thro' & from Milton towards Colle, for the year which began on the 1st day of October last past, & ending the 1st day of October of this present year 1813. the said James Marr —— yielding & paying to the sd Thomas Jefferson five —— Dollars on the 1st day of October closing the year which he covenants to do. and it is further agreed that this lease, & on the same conditions, shall continue from year to year until notice to the contrary be given by either party to the other. Witness their hands this 6th day of February 1813.

witness
E. Bacon

Th: Jefferson
James Marr

LITH. OF SARONY, MAJOR & KNAPP. 449 BROADWAY, N.Y.

"He was just as particular as this with all his business. Whenever I engaged an overseer for him, or any kind of a mechanic, I always made a written contract with him, that stated just what he was to do, and just what pay he was to receive. In this way he avoided all difficulties with the men he employed. I used to write Mr. Jefferson's name so often to contracts that I made for him, that I could imitate his signature almost exactly. A good many people could not tell whether he or I had written his name. Here is one of my contracts with a carpenter, written and signed by myself for Mr. Jefferson:

"'It is agreed between Thomas Jefferson and Richard Durrett, both of the county of Albemarle, that the said Durrett shall serve the said Jefferson one year as a carpenter. And the said Durrett does by these presents oblige himself to do whatever work the said Jefferson shall require in the business of carpenter work; and the said Durrett obliges himself to faithfully do his duty. The year commences on the day that the said Durrett shall take charge of the said Jefferson's employ; for which year's service the said Jefferson agrees to pay the said Durrett forty pounds, and to find him four hundred and fifty pounds of pork, and a peck of corn meal a week; or, in case the said Durrett should have three in family, the said Jefferson agrees to find him three pecks a week, and to find him a cow to give milk from 15th April to 15th November. As witness our hands this 28th of October, 1812.

"'RICHARD DURRETT.

"'E. BACON, for

"'TH. JEFFERSON.'"

Both of the County of Albemarle that the said Durrett
shall serve the said Jefferson one year as a Carp=
=enter. and the said Durrett do by these Presents Oblige him
=self, to do what ever work the said Jefferson shall require
in the Business of Carpenters work and the said Durrett
Obliges himself, to faithfully do his duty the year
commence^d is on the day that the said Durrett shall
take charge of the said Jeffersons imploy. for which years
service the said Jefferson agrees to pay the said Durrett
forty Pounds. and to find him four hundred and fifty
Pounds of Pork and a peck of corn meal a week or.
in case the said Durrett should have three in family
the said Jefferson agrees to find him three pecks a week
and to find him a cow to give milk from 15th April
to 15th November. as witness our hands this 28th October.
1812.

Richard Durrett   E. Bacon for.
Th. Jefferson

LITH. OF SARONY, MAJOR & KNAPP. 449 BROADWAY, N.Y.

CHAPTER VII.

MR. JEFFERSON'S FAMILY.

MR. JEFFERSON'S CHILDREN—MARTHA MARRIED COL. TH. M. RANDOLPH—MARIA MARRIED JOHN W. EPPES, AND DIED YOUNG—MRS. RANDOLPH LIKE HER FATHER IN APPEARANCE, CHARACTER, HABITS, ETC.—MR. JEFFERSON'S INDUSTRY—REMARKABLE STATEMENT—MRS. RANDOLPH'S CHILDREN—THEIR NAMES AND FAMILY CHARACTERISTICS—MR. JEFFERSON'S DEVOTION TO THEM—ADVICE—ANECDOTE—PARTICIPATION IN THEIR SPORTS—VISITS OF SCHOOL CHILDREN TO MONTICELLO—A FIGHT—WILLIAM C. RIVES A PEACE-MAKER—A FINE BOY—GOVERNOR RANDOLPH—HIS ECCENTRICITIES—HIS HORSE "DROMEDARY"—HIS ARREST BY WAGONERS—A BAD MANAGER—SALE OF SLAVES—BILL OF SALE FOR MARIA—HIS TROUBLE TO RAISE MONEY—LETTER—SALE OF EDY—RECEIPT—HIS FAILURE—CHARLES S. BANKHEAD—HIS INTEMPERANCE—CHIVALRY—FIGHT WITH WM. F. GORDON—HIS RECEIPT FOR WINNY AND HER CHILDREN.

"MR. JEFFERSON had four children. Two of them died very young. The other two, Martha and Maria, were in France with him while he was Minister. They were in school there. Martha married Col. Thomas Mann Randolph, afterwards Governor of Virginia. Maria married John W. Eppes. He afterwards went to Congress. He was a very fine-looking man, and a great favorite with everybody. Mrs. Eppes died very young, and was buried at Monticello. She had one boy, Frank Eppes, a fine little fellow. He used to stay at Monticello a good deal.

"I knew Mrs. Randolph as well as I ever knew any person out of my own family. Few such women ever lived. I never saw her equal. I was with Mr. Jefferson twenty years and saw her frequently every week. I never saw her at all out of temper. I can truly say that I never saw two such persons in this respect as she and her father. Sometimes he would refer me to her, or she would refer me to him, a half dozen times in a day. Mrs. Randolph was more like her father than any lady I ever saw. She was nearly as tall as he, and had the same clear, bright complexion, and blue eyes. I have rode over the plantation, I reckon, a thousand times with Mr. Jefferson, and when he was not talking he was nearly always humming some tune, or singing in a low tone to himself. And it was just so with Mrs. Randolph. As she was attending to her duties about the house, she seemed to be always in a happy mood. She had always her father's pleasant smile, and was nearly always humming some tune. I have never seen her at all disturbed by any amount of care and trouble.

Mr. Jefferson was the most industrious person I ever saw in my life. All the time I was with him I had full permission to visit his room whenever I thought it necessary to see him on any business. I knew how to get into his room at any time of day or night. I have sometimes gone into his room when he was in bed, but aside from that I never went into it but twice in the whole twenty years I was with him, that I did not find him employed. I never saw him sitting idle in his room but twice. Once he was suffering with the toothache; and once, in returning from his Bedford farm, he had slept in a room where some of the glass had been broken out of the window, and the wind had blown upon him and given him a kind of neuralgia. At all other times he was either reading, writing, talking, working upon some model, or doing something else.

"Mrs. Randolph was just like her father in this respect. She was always busy. If she wasn't reading or writing, she was always doing something. She used to sit in Mr. Jefferson's room a great deal, and sew, or read, or talk, as he would be busy about something else. As her daughters grew up, she taught them to be industrious like herself. They used to take turns each day in giving out to the servants, and superintending the housekeeping. I knew all her children just as well as I did my own. There were six daughters and five sons. Let me see if I can remember their names. The boys were Thomas Jefferson, James Madison, Benjamin Franklin, Merriweather Lewis, and George Wythe.

The daughters were Anne, Ellen, Virginia, Cornelia, and a little thing that could just run about when I came away. Her name was Septimis, or something like that.* Only two of them were married when I came away. Jeff. married Jane Nicholas, daughter of Gov. Wilson C. Nicholas, and Anne married Charles S. Bankhead. Anne, Ellen, and Merriweather Lewis had the fresh rosy countenance of the Jefferson family. The rest of the family, as far as I can remember—I don't remember about the little ones—had the Randolph complexion, which was dark and Indian-like. You know they claim to be descended from Pocahontas. Virginia and Cornelia were tall, active, and fine-looking, with very dark complexions.

"Mr. Jefferson was perfectly devoted to his grandchildren, and they to him. They delighted to follow him about over the grounds and garden, and he took great pleasure in talking with them, and giving them advice, and directing their sports. I have heard him tell them enough of times that nobody should live without some useful employment. I always raised my boys to work. Mr. Jefferson knew this, and it pleased him. On Saturdays, when they were not in school, they often cut coal wood for the nailery. They could cut a cord a day and earn fifty cents. Governor Ran-

* Septimia.

dolph once told them that if they would cut off the bushes from a certain field, he would give them twenty dollars. His boys would often go and work with them like little Turks on Saturdays, so that my boys could go with them a-fishing. After a while they finished their job and got their pay. Mr. Jefferson heard of it. One evening I heard him talking with his grandchildren about it. He told them my boys had got twenty dollars—more money than any of them had got; that they had earned it themselves, and said a great deal in their praise, and in regard to the importance of industrious habits. Merriweather Lewis was a very bright little fellow. I always thought him the most sprightly of all the Randolph children. He spoke up and said, 'Why, grandpa, if we should work like Fielding and Thomas, our hands would get so rough and sore that we could not hold our books. And we need not work so. We shall be rich, and all we want is a good education, so that we shall be prepared to associate with wealthy and intelligent people.' 'Ah!' said Mr. Jefferson, and I have thought of the remark a thousand times since, 'those that expect to get through the world without industry, because they are rich, will be greatly mistaken. The people that *do* work will soon get possession of all their property.' I have heard him give those children a great deal of good advice. I remember, once, hearing him tell them that they should never laugh in a loud, boisterous manner in company, or in the presence of strangers. That was his own habit.

"He took great pleasure in the sports and plays of his grandchildren. I have often seen him direct them and enjoy them greatly. The large lawn back of the house was a fine place for their plays. They very often ran races, and he would give the word for them to start, and decide who was the winner. Another play was stealing goods. They would divide into two parties, and lay down their coats, hats, knives, and other things, and each party would try to get all that the other had. If they were caught in the attempt to steal they were made prisoners. I have seen Mr. Jefferson laugh heartily to see this play go on. The children about the country used to enjoy coming there. It was a fine place for them to play, and in the fruit season there was always the greatest quantities of good fruit. Jeff. Randolph used very often to bring his school-mates there.

"Before the University of Virginia was established, a man of the name of Oglesby taught a school at Charlottesville. I think he was a Scotch-man. I know he was a foreigner. He was a fine teacher, and had a very large school. Thomas Jefferson Randolph, Wm. C. Rives, Walker Gilmore, Vaul W. Southall, Wm. F. Gordon, and a host of other boys went to his school. Almost every Friday evening Jeff. Randolph would bring a lot of his mates to Monticello to play and eat fruit. If they did not come on Friday they were pretty certain to come on Saturday. I gave them the keys of the house and garden, and very often they all stayed there over night. One Saturday a lot of the schoolboys that were not invited concluded that they would come also, and help themselves to fruit. They went around the back side of the garden, broke off the palings, and got in. They then climbed the trees and broke off a good many limbs, and did a great deal of damage. The other party attacked them, and they had a tremendous fight. The party that had broken in was much the largest, and they could not drive them off. They threw stones at the old gardener and hurt him very badly. They sent to the mill for me, and when I got there the other party were gone, and some of Jeff.'s party were a good deal hurt. Vaul Southall was very bloody. He had fought like a little tiger. Wm. C. Rives was one of Jeff.'s party. He was an uncommonly fine boy, and was always the peacemaker among the boys. Whenever they got into a difficulty among themselves, they would all say, 'Let Willie Rives settle it.' Both parties were always willing to select him as umpire. So I said to him, 'Willie, why didn't you settle this matter without all this fighting?' He was very much excited, as well as all the rest of them. 'Why, sir,' said he, 'you know that I am a little fellow and couldn't do much fighting, but I called them all the hard names I could think of, and then I started to turn Rompo loose on them, and they all ran off.' Rompo was a very fierce dog. I should like very much to see Wm. C. Rives now. I suppose he is quite an old man, though I was a man grown when he was a little boy. He was at Monticello a great deal. Very often he did not like the doings of the other boys, when I gave them the keys to stay up there alone, and he would come down and stay all night at my house. He has stayed there many a night. The other boys were too intimate with the negro women to suit him. He was always a very modest boy. I once heard one of the other boys make a vulgar remark. He said, 'Such talk as that ought not to be thought, much less spoken out.' Mr. Jefferson thought a great deal of him, and so did all the family. I think it would have suited them all mighty well if he had married Ellen. But I don't think he ever courted her, and I don't know that she would have married him if he had. He got in love with Miss Walker and married her. I remember Ellen was one day at my house, and my wife was joking her about him, telling her what a fine thing it would be, he was such a fine young man, and had such a large property. After a while she said, 'Oh, he is too much of a runt to make anybody a husband,' and ran off as fast as she could.

"Gov. Randolph, Mr. Jefferson's son-in-law, was a very eccentric man, and would often do the most strange and laughable things. I remember, once, going with him to Edgehill, his plantation, to look after the hands that were at work in the harvest-field, cutting and putting up the wheat. He looked at the shocks, and a good many of them were not put up to suit him. He was riding 'Dromedary.' Suddenly he dashed away and rode him right through a large number of the shocks, scattering them in all directions. We then rode on to where the overseer was engaged with the hands. After getting through with all his business with the overseer, as he was leaving he told him he thought the old bull must have been in the lot; he had seen a good many shocks torn down and scattered about as he came along. The overseer looked at me and laughed. He understood the matter perfectly.

"The main road from the western part of the State to Richmond ran between Monticello and Edgehill. There was always a great deal of hauling on that road, and teams were almost constantly passing. They got in the habit of camping in the lane just beyond Mr. Randolph's house, and burnt his rails, and made him a heap of trouble. He sent his overseer one night to remonstrate with them against burning his rails. There were a large number of them, and they just laughed at him, and finally gave him a tremendous whipping. When Mr. Randolph heard of it he said he would go himself next time. He was tall, swarthy, and rawboned—one of the stoutest men I ever saw, and afraid of nothing. He was generally dressed in the most indifferent manner, and was very queer any way. The Randolphs were all strange people. John Randolph, you know, was one of the most eccentric men that ever lived, and I think Gov. Randolph was full out as strange a man as he. They were as much alike as any two steers you ever saw.

"A few nights after the overseer was whipped, they camped again, built their fires, were cooking their supper, and Gov. Randolph went down to see them. They soon discovered him, creeping about very slyly and watching them, and thought it was somebody trying to steal their horses. They were often troubled in this way; negroes and others would get their horses and ride them off, and they would have a great deal of trouble to find them in the morning. At length they gave chase, and he allowed himself to be very easily taken. They accused him of trying to steal their horses, said they would have him punished, and demanded that he should tell them where a magistrate lived. He pointed to his own house, and told them that a magistrate lived there. Two of them led him to it. It was the strangest-looking house you ever saw, as strange as himself. They led him into the piazza, and he told them he would go in and get the magistrate. He soon reappeared with his pistols, let them know he had brought them to his own house, stormed at them with his big grum voice in the roughest manner until he had scared them sufficiently, and then very calmly told them to be careful whom they arrested hereafter, gave them some good advice, and sent them away. I knew one of those wagoners very well. He used often to tell of it, and laugh at the way they were taken in by the Governor.

"Governor Randolph was a very hard rider. It was a very common thing with him when he was Governor to start from Richmond after supper and ride 'Dromedary' home by daylight next morning. He would do strange things with that horse. They were just suited to each other. I have often seen him take hold of his tail and run him up the mountain as hard as he could go.

"Mr. Jefferson, Mr. Randolph and I were once riding up the mountain together, and we overtook an old bald-headed negro, who did nothing but haul wood and water. 'Isaac,' said Mr. Randolph, with his big grum voice, 'have you got any tobacco?' 'Yes, master,' said he, taking off his hat and making a low bow with a great flourish, and handed him the tobacco out of the top of his hat. Mr. Jefferson laughed and said, 'It comes from a very shining place.'

"Governor Randolph was a very poor manager. He often had to sell off negroes to pay his debts. Here is a bill of sale for a woman I bought of him. She belonged to an excellent family of servants. He wished me to take another woman instead of her, but I preferred her decidedly, and would not do it, and, as he was obliged to raise the money, he let me have her.

"'BILL OF SALE.

"'I hereby convey to Edmund Bacon, for the sum of five hundred dollars, namely, in cash five hundred dollars, and in his note of hand $ due on demand, a full and indefeasible right, title, and estate in a female slave, Maria, daughter of Iris, born at Edgehill, this day put into his possession, and I, for myself, my heirs, executors, administrators, &c., the said title to the said slave do forever warrant and defend to the said Bacon, his heirs or

... for the sum of five hundred Dollars viz.
in cash five hundd dollrs and in his Note of hand 0 $. 0 cts
due on demand, a full and indefeazible right
title and Estate in a female Slave Maria daugh-
-ter of his, born at Edgehill, this day put into his
possession, and I for myself, my heirs, Exrs Admrs
&c. the said title to the said Slave do forever
warrant and defend to the said Edmd. Bacon his
heirs or assigns: . Witness my hand & seal
this Oct. 9th. 1818.

Done in presence
of

Dan. Colclaser

William F. Gordon

James O. Walker —

Th M Randolph [seal]

LITH. OF SARONY, MAJOR & KNAPP. 449 BROADWAY. N.Y.

Dear Sir,

It is so absolutely ne--cessary to me to have as much as 150 $ by tomorrow evening to send by express to pay into the Bank of U.S. and Bank of Virginia in Richmond, before 3 o'clock on Wednesday next, that I am forced, against my will, to impor-tune your father with the offer of the little girl at Edgehill. Do you think it would be possible for us to borrow that money between us by 3 o'clock tomorrow? I should have set off down today, but the hope of succeeding to--morrow so as to do by sending, has stoped me. I am obliged to be in Richmond on the Board of Public Works Week after next and my presence is more wanted now at Edgehill than Varina. Besides my Wife is really ill today. Could you prevail on your Mother to lend as much money?

Your friend

Mr Bacon.

ThM Randolph

May 9. 1819.

assigns. Witness my hand and seal this October 9th, 1818.

"'TH. M. RANDOLPH. [SEAL.]

"'Done in presence of

"'DANIEL CALDASE,

"'WILLIAM F. CARDIN,

"'JAMES O. WALLERS.'

[*See Facsimile.*]

"While he was Governor his debts troubled him a great deal. I often loaned him money, and he often applied to me to help him raise it from others. When he must have it, and could get it in no other way, he would be obliged to sell some of his negroes. Here is one of his letters to me.

"It is superscribed:

"'MR. EDM. BACON, by PHIL.

"'DEAR SIR: It is so absolutely necessary to me to have as much as $150 by to-morrow evening, to send by express to pay into the Bank of U. S., and Bank of Virginia in Richmond, before 3 o'clock on Wednesday next, that I am forced, against my will, to importune you farther with the offer of the little girl at Edgehill. Do you think it would be possible for us to borrow that money between us by 3 o'clock to-morrow? I should have set off down to-day, but the hope of succeeding to-morrow so as to do by sending, has stopped me. I am obliged to be in Richmond on the Board of Public Works week after next, and my presence is more wanted now at Edgehill than Varina. Besides, my wife is really ill to-day. Could you prevail on your mother to lend as much money?

"'Your friend,

"'TH. M. RANDOLPH.

"'MR. BACON. *May* 9, 1819.'

[*See Facsimile.*]

"I raised the money for him, and the next day paid him two hundred dollars for Edy. She was a little girl four years old. He gave me this receipt:

"'Received from Edmund Bacon two hundred dollars for Edy, daughter of Fennel, now at Edgehill, and I bind myself to make a complete title in the said Edy to the said Bacon. Witness my hand, this May 16, 1819.

"'TH. M. RANDOLPH.'

[*See Facsimile.*]

"He was finally unable to meet his obligations, failed completely, and lost every thing. Mr. Jefferson, in making his will,* had to take especial care to prevent Mr. Randolph's creditors from getting what property he left for Mrs. Randolph.

---

* See Mr. Jefferson's Will in the Appendix.

Received from Edmund Bacon two hundred Dollars for Edy the daughter of Fennell now at Edgehill and I bind myself to make a complete title in the said Edy to the said Bacon

Witness my hand
this May 10. 1819

Th M Randolph

Teste

LITH. OF SARONY, MAJOR & KNAPP. 449 BROADWAY. N.Y.

"Before he died his mind became shattered, and he pretty much lost his reason. He had no control of his temper. I have seen him cane his son Jeff. after he was a grown man. Jeff. made no resistance, but got away from him as soon as he could. I have seen him knock down his son-in-law Charles L. Bankhead with an iron poker. Bankhead married his daughter Anne. She was a perfectly lovely woman. She was a Jefferson in temper. He was the son of a very wealthy man who lived near Fredericksburg. He was a fine-looking man, but a terrible drunkard. I have seen him ride his horse into the bar-room at Charlottesville and get a drink of liquor. I have seen his wife run from him when he was drunk and hide in a potato-hole to get out of danger. He once stabbed Jeff. Randolph because he had said something about his abuse of his sister, and I think would have killed him, if I had not interfered and separated them.

"One night he was very drunk and made a great disturbance, because Burwell, who kept the keys, would not give him any more brandy. Mrs. Randolph could not manage him, and she sent for me. She would never call on Mr. Randolph at such a time, he was so excitable. But he heard the noise in the dining-room and rushed in to see what was the matter. He entered the room just as I did, and Bankhead, thinking he was Burwell, began to curse him. Seizing an iron poker that was standing by the fireplace, he knocked him down as quick as I ever saw a bullock fall. The blow pealed the skin off one side of his forehead and face, and he bled terribly. It if had been a square blow, instead of glancing off as it did, it must have killed him.

"Bankhead came to me one Court day at Charlottesville and told me he did not want me and one of our overseers that was with me to leave him that day. He did not tell us what he wanted, and we had no idea. We saw that he did not get drunk that day as usual, and we were surprised at that. Towards night he came to us and said he wanted us to start home with him. We rode out of town some distance towards Monticello, and he got off his horse and hitched him to the fence, and requested us to hitch ours and stay with him. We still had no idea of what he was about, or what he wanted of us. At length Phil. Barbour and Wm. F. Gordon rode along. Gordon had been employed in a suit against Bankhead, and in making his speech he had taken a lawyer's privilege and said a good many severe things about him, for which he had determined to fight him. Bankhead went out immediately in front of Gordon and requested him to get down; said he wanted to speak to him. Gordon made some excuse, and declined. Bankhead asked him again, and Gordon, who seemed to have no idea what he wanted, gave some reason that I have forgotten, and again declined. Bankhead then told him he had insulted him, and began to curse him with all his might. He told him that he was armed, and that if he did not get down, he would bring him down—he would shoot him; 'but,' said he, 'if you will get down, I will throw away my pistols, and agree to fight you with nothing but what my mother gave me.' It was no use for Gordon to refuse, nor for us to try to prevent the fight. He got off his horse, and he had hardly touched the ground, before at it they went, and I never in all my life saw such a fight. They fought and fought, and neither seemed to get the least bit of advantage over the other. They clinched several times, and tried to throw each other down, but both were too strong and supple. Neither could get the other down. I never did see as even a match. I think they must have fought a half an hour, and both of them were as bloody as butchers, when I told Phil. Barbour it would never do for us to let them fight any longer—we must separate them. So he took hold of Gordon, and I took hold of Bankhead, and we just pulled them apart.

"Bankhead got the worst of it. One eye was badly injured, and I think never did get entirely over the hurt. Bankhead was the stoutest, but

Gordon had the best wind. I often heard him describe the fight, and laugh about it afterwards. He said he thought of crying 'Enough!' several times, but Bankhead kept him so busy he hadn't time.

"I bought a negro woman and her two children of Bankhead. Here is his receipt:

"'This writing proves that I have sold and received payment for a negro woman named Winny, and her two children, and that I promise and am bound to give a bill of sale for s'd negro's, having received payment.

"'As witness my hand, &c.

"'CHAS. L. BANKHEAD.

"'Test,

"'THOS. WELLS.

"'1*st July*, 1814.'"

[*See Facsimile.*]

sold & recieved payment for a
a negro woman named [illegible]
and her two children, and that
I promise, and am bound to
to give a bill of sale for
the negro's having recd
payment

as witness my hand

Chs: L Bankhead

1st July 1814

Test.

CHAPTER VIII.

MR. JEFFERSON'S SERVANTS.

MR. JEFFERSON AN INDULGENT MASTER—NOT WILLING TO HAVE HIS SERVANTS OVERWORKED, OR WHIPPED—NAILS STOLEN BY JIM HUBBARD—HIS PENITENCE AND FORGIVENESS—FAVORITE SERVANTS—THE HOUSE SERVANTS—IN THE ROOM WHEN MRS. JEFFERSON DIED—HIS PROMISE NOT TO MARRY AGAIN—MR. JEFFERSON'S INSTRUCTIONS IN REGARD TO HIS CIDER—SALLY HEMINGS CROSSED THE OCEAN WITH MARIA JEFFERSON—THEIR STAY IN LONDON WITH MRS. ADAMS—MRS. ADAMS' LETTERS—URSULA, JOHN HEMINGS, JOE FOSSET—A FUGITIVE SLAVE—SERVANTS FREED BY MR. JEFFERSON—HIS VIEWS OF SLAVERY.

"MR. JEFFERSON was always very kind and indulgent to his servants. He would not allow them to be at all overworked, and he would hardly ever allow one of them to be whipped. His orders to me were constant, that if there was any servant that could not be got along with without the chastising that was customary, to dispose of him. He could not bear to have a servant whipped, no odds how much he deserved it. I remember one case in particular. Mr. Jefferson gave written instructions that I should always sell the nails that were made in his nailery. We made from sixpenny to twenty-penny nails, and always kept a supply of each kind on hand. I went one day to supply an order, and the eight-penny nails were all gone, and there was a full supply of all the other sizes. Of course they had been stolen. I soon became satisfied that Jim Hubbard, one of the servants that worked in the nailery, had stolen them, and charged him with it. He denied it powerfully. I talked with Grady, the overseer of the nailery, about it, and finally I said, 'Let us drop it. He has hid them somewhere, and if we say no more about it, we shall find them.' I examined his house, and every place I could think of, but for some time I could find nothing of the nails. One day after a rain, as I was following a path through the woods, I saw muddy tracks on the leaves leading off from the path. I followed them until I came to a tree-top, where I found the nails buried in a large box. There were several hundred pounds of them. From circumstances, I knew that Jim had stolen them. Mr. Jefferson was at home at the time, and when I went up to Monticello I told him of it. He was very much surprised, and felt very badly about it. Jim had always been a favorite servant. He told me to be at my house next morning when he took his ride, and he would see Jim there. When he came, I sent for Jim, and I never saw any person, white or black, feel as badly as he did when he saw his master. He was mortified and distressed beyond measure. He had been brought up in the shop, and we all had confidence in him. Now his character was gone. The tears streamed down his face, and he begged pardon over and over again. I felt very badly myself. Mr. Jefferson turned to me, and said, 'Ah, sir, we can't punish him. He has suffered enough already.' He then talked to him, gave him a heap of good advice, and sent him to the shop. Grady had waited, expecting to be sent for to whip him, and he was astonished to see him come back and go to work after such a crime. When he came to dinner—he boarded with me then—he told me, that when Jim came back to the shop, he said, 'Well, I'se been a-seeking religion a long time, but I never heard any thing before that sounded so, or made me feel so, as I did when master said, "Go, and don't do so any more;" and now I'se determined to seek religion till I find it;' and sure enough, he afterwards came to me for a permit to go and be baptized. I gave him one, and never knew of his doing any thing of the sort again. He was always a good servant afterwards

"Mr. Jefferson had a large number of favorite servants, that were treated just as well as could be. Burwell was the main, principal servant on the place. He did not go to Washington. Mr. Jefferson had the most perfect confidence in him. He told me not to be at all particular with him—to let him do pretty much as he pleased, and to let him have pocket money occasionally, as he wanted it.

"Once or twice every week while Mr. Jefferson was President, I opened every room in the house, and had it thoroughly aired. When I was so busy that I could not attend to this myself, I would send the keys to Burwell, and he would air the house, and was, if possible, more particular than I was. He stayed at Monticello, and took charge of the meat-house, garden, &c., and kept the premises in order. Mr. Jefferson gave him his freedom in his will, and it was right that he should do it.

"The house servants were Betty Brown, Sally, Critta, and Betty Hemings, Nance, and Ursula. They were old family servants, and great favorites. They were in the room when Mrs. Jefferson died.* She died before I went to live with him, and left four little children. He never married again. They have often told my wife, that when Mrs. Jefferson died, they stood around the bed. Mr. Jefferson sat by her, and she gave him directions about a good many things that she wanted done. When she came to the children, she wept, and could not speak for some time. Finally she held up her hand, and spreading out her four fingers, she told him she

* Mrs. Jefferson died in 1782.

could not die happy if she thought her four children were ever to have a step-mother brought in over them. Holding her other hand in his, Mr. Jefferson promised her solemnly that he would never marry again. And he never did. He was then quite a young man, and very handsome, and I suppose he could have married well; but he always kept that promise.

"These women remained at Monticello while he was President. I was instructed to take no control of them. They had very little to do. When I opened the house, they attended to airing it. Then every March we had to bottle all his cider. Dear me, this was a job. It took us two weeks. Mr. Jefferson was very particular about his cider. He gave me instructions to have every apple cleaned perfectly clean when it was made. Here are his instructions:

"'We have saved red Hughes enough from the north orchard to make a smart cask of cyder. They are now mellow, and beginning to rot. I will pray you, therefore, to have them made into cyder immediately. Let them be made clean one by one, and all the rotten ones thrown away, or the rot cut out. Nothing else can ensure good cyder.'

"Sally Hemings went to France with Maria

Jefferson when she was a little girl. Mr. Jefferson was Minister to France, and he wanted to put her in school there. They crossed the ocean alone. I have often heard her tell about it. When they got to London, they stayed with Mr. Adams, who was Minister there, until Mr. Jefferson came or sent for them. I have read a beautiful letter that Mrs. Adams wrote to her sister, Mrs. Cranch, about her. Here it is:

"'I have had with me for a fortnight a little daughter of Mr. Jefferson's, who arrived here with a young negro girl, her servant, from Virginia. Mr. Jefferson wrote me some months ago that he expected them, and desired me to receive them. I did so, and was amply repaid for my trouble. A finer child of her age I never saw. So mature an understanding, so womanly a behavior, and so much sensibility, united, are rarely to be met with. I grew so fond of her, and she was so attached to me, that, when Mr. Jefferson sent for her, they were obliged to force the little creature away. She is but eight years old. She would sit, sometimes, and describe to me the parting with her aunt, who brought her up, the obligations she was under to her, and the love she had for her little cousins, till the tears would stream down her cheeks; and how I had been her friend, and she loved me. Her papa would break her heart by making her go again. She clung round me so that I could not help shedding a tear at parting with her. She was the favorite of every one in the house. I regret that such fine spirits must be spent in the walls of a convent. She is a beautiful girl, too.' *

"Ursula was Mrs. Randolph's nurse. She was a big fat woman. She took charge of all the children that were not in school. If there was any switching to be done, she always did it. She used to be down at my house a great deal with those children. They used to be there so much, that we very often got tired of them; but we never said so. They were all very much attached to their nurse. They always called her 'Mammy.'

"John Hemings was a carpenter. He was a first-rate workman—a very extra workman. He could make any thing that was wanted in wood-work. He learned his trade of Dinsmore. He made most of the wood-work of Mr. Jefferson's fine carriage. Joe Fosset made the iron-work. He was a very fine workman; could do any thing it was necessary to do with steel or iron. He learned his trade of Stewart. Mr. Jefferson kept Stewart several years longer than he would otherwise have done, in order that his own servants might learn

* Mrs. Adams' Letters, vol. ii., p. 179.

his trade thoroughly. Stewart was a very superior workman, but he would drink. And Burwell was a fine painter. He painted the carriage, and always kept the house painted. He painted a good deal at the University.

"Mr. Jefferson freed a number of his servants in his will. I think he would have freed all of them, if his affairs had not been so much involved that he could not do it. He freed one girl some years before he died, and there was a great deal of talk about it. She was nearly as white as anybody, and very beautiful. People said he freed her because she was his own daughter. She was not his daughter; she was ......'s daughter. I know that. I have seen him come out of her mother's room many a morning, when I went up to Monticello very early. When she was nearly grown, by Mr. Jefferson's direction I paid her stage fare to Philadelphia, and gave her fifty dollars. I have never seen her since, and don't know what became of her. From the time she was large enough, she always worked in the cotton factory. She never did any hard work.

"While Mr. Madison was President, one of our slaves ran away, and we never got him again. As soon as I learned that he was gone, I was satisfied that he had gone with Mr. Madison's cart to Washington, and had passed himself off as Mr. Madison's servant. But Jeff. Randolph did not believe it. He believed he had hid himself somewhere about the plantation, and he hunted everywhere for him. Finally he said he was sure he was hid in the loft of the stable where we kept our mules. I told him it was no use to look; but he would do it, and while crawling over the hay-mow, he tumbled through. I thought the mules would tread or kick him to death, but when he came out he said the mules were as badly scared as he was, when he fell among them, and did not move or hurt him at all. We afterwards learned that he went off with Mr. Madison's servant, as I had supposed. No servants ever had a kinder master than Mr. Jefferson's. He did not like slavery. I have heard him talk a great deal about it. He thought it a bad system. I have heard him prophesy that we should have just such trouble with it as we are having now.*

---

* Capt. Bacon is a stanch Union man, utterly opposed to the whole secession movement.

CHAPTER IX.

MR. JEFFERSON AT WASHINGTON—HIS LIBRARY.

CAPT. BACON'S VISITS TO MR JEFFERSON IN WASHINGTON—APPEARANCE OF THE CITY—THE PRESIDENT'S HOUSE—ITS DOMESTIC ARRANGEMENTS—SERVANTS FROM MONTICELLO—STEWARD—COOK—CARRIAGE DRIVER—VISITORS—DINNERS—MARKET—EXPENSE—MOVING HOME MR. JEFFERSON'S GOODS AND SERVANTS—SNOW-STORM—CAPT. BACON MISTAKEN FOR THE PRESIDENT—MR. JEFFERSON'S RECEPTION ON THE WAY—ANXIETY TO SEE "OLD TOM"—HIS RECEPTION AT HOME—HIS LIBRARY—SALE TO CONGRESS—REMOVAL TO WASHINGTON—SIXTEEN WAGON LOADS—HIS LOUNGE—WRITING-TABLE—BIBLE-READING—CHANCELLOR WYTHE'S LIBRARY.

"I VISITED Mr. Jefferson at Washington three times while he was President. My first visit was soon after his inauguration. I went to take his carriage horses. The second time I went he had got very much displeased with two of his servants, Davy and Fanny, and he wished me to take them to Alexandria and sell them. They were married, and had got into a terrible quarrel. Davy was jealous of his wife, and, I reckon, with good reason. When I got there, they learned what I had come for, and they were in great trouble. They wept, and begged, and made good promises, and made such an ado, that they begged the old gentleman out of it. But it was a good lesson for them. I never heard any more complaint of them; and when I left Mr. Jefferson, I left them both at Monticello.

"The last time I visited Mr. Jefferson in Washington, I stayed there sixteen days. This was when I went to help him settle up his business, and move home his goods and servants. He had eleven servants with him from Monticello. He had a French cook in Washington named Julien, and he took Eda and Fanny there, to learn French cookery. He always preferred French cookery. Eda and Fanny were afterwards his cooks at Monticello.

"Some days I was very busy attending to packing up his goods, getting in his bills, and settling up his business. Other days I had very little to do, and I would go up to the Capitol. I haven't been in Washington since the British played the wild there in the war of 1812. When I was there, the President's house was surrounded with a high rock wall, and there was an iron gate immediately in front of it, and from that gate to the Capitol the street was just as straight as a gun-barrel. Nearly all the houses were on that street. I took a great deal of pleasure in going to the Capitol and hearing the debates.

"Mr. Jefferson often told me that the office of Vice-President was far preferable to that of President. He was perfectly tired out with company. He had a very long dining-room, and his table was chock-full every one of the sixteen days I was there. There were Congressmen, foreigners, and all sorts of people to dine with him. He dined at four o'clock, and they generally sat and talked until night. It used to worry me to sit so long, and I finally quit when I got through eating, and went off and left them.

"The first thing in the morning there, was to go to market. There was no market then in Washington. Mr. Jefferson's steward was a Frenchman named Lamar. He was a very smart man, was well educated, and as much of a gentleman in his appearance as any man. His carriage driver was an Irishman named Dougherty. He would get out the wagon early in the morning, and Lamar would go with him to Georgetown to market. I have all my life been in the habit of getting up about four o'clock in the morning, and I went with them very often. Lamar told me that it often took fifty dollars to pay for what marketing they would use in a day. Mr. Jefferson's salary did not support him while he was President.

"We got loaded up ready to start home, and I left Washington on the third of March. Mr. Jefferson stayed to attend the inauguration, but overtook us before we got home. I had three wagons from Monticello—two six-mule teams loaded with boxes, and the other four sorrel Chickasaw horses, and the wagon pretty much loaded with shrubbery from Maine's nursery. The servants rode on these wagons. I had the carriage horses and carriage, and rode behind them.

"On our way home we had a tremendous snowstorm. It snowed very fast, and when we reached Culpepper Court House it was half-leg deep. A large crowd of people had collected there, expecting that the President would be along. When I rode up, they thought I was the President, and shouted and hurrahed tremendously. When I got out of the carriage, they laughed very heartily at their mistake. There was a platform along the whole front of the tavern, and it was full of people. Some of them had been waiting a good while, and drinking a good deal, and they made so much noise that they scared the horses, and Diomede backed, and tread upon my foot, and lamed me so that I could hardly get into the carriage the next morning. There was one very tall old fellow that was noisier than any of the rest, who said he was bound to see the President—'Old Tom,' he called him. They asked me when he would be along, and I told them I thought he would certainly be along that night, and I looked for him every moment. The tavern was kept by an old man named Shackleford. I told him to have a large fire built in a private room, as Mr. Jefferson would be very cold when he got there, and he did so. I soon heard shouting, went out, and Mr. Jefferson was in sight. He was in a one-horse vehicle—a phaeton—with a driver, and a servant on horseback. When he came up, there was great cheering again. I motioned to him to follow me; took him straight to his room, and locked the door. The tall old fellow came and knocked very often, but I would not let him in. I told Mr. Jefferson not to mind him, he was drunk. Finally the door was opened, and they rushed in and filled the room. It was as full as I ever saw a bar-room. He stood up, and made a short address to them. Afterwards some of them told him how they had mistaken me for him. He went on next day, and reached Monticello before we did, so that I did not see the large reception that the people of Albemarle gave him when he got home.*

---

* Mr. Jefferson was present at the inauguration of his successor, and soon afterwards set out for home. The inhabitants of the county of his birth and residence (Albemarle) had proposed to meet and escort him to Monticello, with imposing ceremonies. He quietly put aside the request, by declaring that he could not decide on the day of his return, and he added:

"Mr. Jefferson d a very large library. When the British burnt Washington, the library that belonged to Congress was destroyed, and Mr. Jeffer-

---

"But it is a sufficient happiness to me to know that my fellow-citizens of the country generally entertain for me the kind sentiments which have prompted this proposition, without giving to so many the trouble of leaving their homes to meet a single individual. I shall have opportunities of taking them individually by the hand at our Court House and other public places, and of exchanging assurances of mutual esteem. Certainly it is the greatest consolation to me to know, that in returning to the bosom of my native county, I shall be again in the midst of their kind affections; and I can say with truth that my return to them will make me happier than I have been since I left them."

The proposed ovation gave way to an address, and it was thus answered:

"To the Inhabitants of Albemarle County, in Virginia.

"April 3, 1809.

"Returning to the scenes of my birth and early life, to the society of those with whom I was raised, and who have been ever dear to me, I receive, fellow-citizens and neighbors, with inexpressible pleasure, the cordial welcome you are so good as to give me. Long absent on duties which the history of a wonderful era made incumbent on those called to them, the pomp, the turmoil, the bustle and splendor of office, have drawn but deeper sighs for the tranquil and irresponsible occupations of private life, for the enjoyment of an affectionate intercourse with you, my neighbors and friends, and the endearments of family love, which nature has given us all, as the sweetener of every hour. For these I gladly lay down the distressing burden of power, and seek, with my fellow-citizens, repose and safety under the watchful cares, and labors, and perplexities, of younger and abler minds. The anxieties you express to administer to my happiness, do, of themselves, confer that happiness; and the

son sold them his. He directed me to have it packed in boxes and sent to Washington. John Hemings, one of his servants, made the boxes, and Burwell and I packed them up mostly. Dinsmore helped us some, and the girls, Ellen, Virginia, and Cornelia would come in sometimes and sort them out, and help us a good deal. There was an immense quantity of them. There were sixteen wagon loads. I engaged the teams. Each wagon was to carry three thousand pounds for a load, and to have four dollars a day for delivering them in Washington. If they carried more than three thousand pounds, they were to have extra pay. There were all kinds of books—books in a great many languages that I knew nothing about. There were a great many religious books among them—

---

measure will be complete, if my endeavors to fulfil my duties in the several public stations to which I have been called, have obtained for me the approbation of my country. The part which I have acted on the theatre of public life, has been before them, and to their sentence I submit it; but the testimony of my native county, of the individuals who have known me in private life, to my conduct in its various duties and relations, is the more grateful, as proceeding from eye-witnesses, and observers, from triers of the vicinage. Of you, then, my neighbors, I may ask, in the face of the world, "Whose ox have I taken, or whom have I defrauded? Whom have I oppressed, or of whose hand have I received a bribe to blind mine eyes therewith?" On your verdict I rest with conscious security. Your wishes for my happiness are received with just sensibility, and I offer sincere prayers for your own welfare and prosperity."

[RANDALL'S LIFE OF JEFFERSON, vol. iii., pp. 305, 306.]

more than I have ever seen anywhere else. All the time Mr. Jefferson was President I had the keys to his library, and I could go in and look over the books, and take out any one that I wished, and read and return it. I have written a good many letters from that library to Mr. Jefferson in Washington. Mr. Jefferson had a sofa or lounge upon which he could sit or recline, and a small table on rollers, upon which he could write, or lay his books. Sometimes he would draw this table up before the sofa, and sit and read or write; and other times he would recline on his sofa, with his table rolled up the sofa, astride it. He had a large Bible, which nearly always lay at the head of his sofa. Many and many a time I have gone into his room and found him reading that Bible. You remember I told you about riding all night from Richmond, after selling that flour, and going into his room very early in the morning, and paying over to him the new United States Bank money. *That* was one of the times that I found him with the big Bible open before him on his little table, and he busy reading it. And I have seen him reading it in that way many a time. Some people, you know, say he was an atheist. Now if he was an atheist, what did he want with all those religious books, and why did he spend so much of his time reading his Bible?

"When Chancellor Wythe died, he willed to Mr. Jefferson his library. It was very large, and nearly filled up the room of the one he sold to Congress. Mr. Jefferson studied law with Chancellor Wythe. They thought a great deal of each other.

CHAPTER X.

MR. JEFFERSON'S HOSPITALITY.

HIS VISITORS—MR. MADISON—HIS APPEARANCE AND CHARACTER—MR. MONROE—HIS ABILITY—LETTERS—A BAD MANAGER—WHAT MADE HIM PRESIDENT—THE THREE EX-PRESIDENTS TOGETHER—OTHER VISITORS CAME IN GANGS—THEIR HORSES, AND WHAT THEY CONSUMED—MRS. RANDOLPH'S TROUBLE TO ENTERTAIN THEM—MR. JEFFERSON'S REASON FOR GOING TO POPLAR FOREST—REASONS OF HIS FAILURE—GOV. WILSON C. NICHOLAS—THOMAS J. RANDOLPH—REASONS FOR LEAVING MR. JEFFERSON—THE PARTING—SUBSEQUENT CORRESPONDENCE—CAPT. BACON'S OPINION OF MR. JEFFERSON—CONCLUSION.

"MR. JEFFERSON always had a great deal of company. He enjoyed seeing his friends very much. Mr. Madison was very often at Monticello. He generally stayed there when he attended Court at Charlottesville. He was a fine man. He had a very solid look. I always thought he looked like a Methodist preacher; he wore his hair as they did then. Mr. Monroe, too, was at Monticello a great deal. I have seen him hundreds of times, and done a great deal of business with him. I sold him the nails, from Mr. Jefferson's nailery, for his house. I have had a great many letters from him. He was a miserable writer. Mr. Jefferson and Mr. Madison both wrote a plain, beautiful hand, but you could write better with your toes than Mr. Monroe wrote. I have heard Governor Morris say, that once, after Mr. Monroe had transcribed a paper, he could not read it. (Laughed heartily.) Here are two of Mr. Monroe's letters:

"'Sir,—There has been a mistake in the kind of nails which I have written for. I cannot say whether you or I have made it. I wanted sixteen-penny nails, and eightpenny. Mr. Fogg will want some of the latter kind for his hog'ds, which I will thank you to add to those already written for.

"'I expect to pay you the cash at Court, or to make an arrangement to suit you.

"'Your very obedient servant,

"'Jas. Monroe.

"'Mr. Bacon.

"'*January* 8, 1810.'

[*See Facsimile.*]

"'Sir,—I have rec'd, by the boy, three pounds nineteen and seven pence, the balance due me of the fifty dollars sent you this morning, after paying £11 0*s.* 5*d.* due Mr. Jefferson for nails. The statement is perfectly correct, and I am happy that it was in my power to accommodate you with the money.

"'I am respectfully yours,

"'Jas. Monroe.

"'*Feb.* 7, 1810.'

Sir

There has been a mistake in the kind of nails which I have written for, I can not say whether you or I have made it. I wanted sixteen penny nails & eight penny. Mr Bogg will want some of the latter kind for his negroes. which I will thank you to add to those already written for.

I expect to pay you the cash at court or to make an arrangement to suit you. yr very obt servt.

Jas Monroe

Jany 28. 1810.

Mr Bacon

LITH. OF SARONY, MAJOR & KNAPP, 449 BROADWAY, N.Y.

"Mr. Monroe was an indifferent manager—was nearly always in debt. He once applied to me to oversee for him, and offered me more than Mr. Jefferson was paying me; but I said, 'Sir, I would not leave Mr. Jefferson for any price.' 'Then,' said he, 'you must help me to get a man. You know what I want.' I recommended a man to him, and he employed him.

"Mr. Monroe was not the equal of Mr. Jefferson or Mr. Madison; and Chapman Johnson, Vaul W. Southall, Wm. F. Gordon, and Phil. Barbour were enough better lawyers than he. Everybody knew that. But he made the purchase of Louisiana, and that made him President. It was thought that he managed that matter remarkably well. I well remember the firing of guns and great rejoicings there were when the news of that purchase first came. It made Mr. Monroe so popular, that he was elected President almost without opposition.

"It used to be very interesting to the people to see the three ex-Presidents together. I have often seen them meet at Charlottesville on Court day, and stand and talk together a few minutes, and crowds of people would gather around them and listen to their conversation, and follow them wherever they would go. I remember one Court day I had been helping Scott, the Kentucky drover, sell his mules, as I knew all the people. He made fine sales that day, and when he had got through, he felt remarkably well, and insisted on treating the company. When he came out of the bar-room he saw a large crowd collected together, and wanted to know what it meant. I told him Mr. Jefferson, Mr. Madison, and Mr. Monroe were there. 'The three Virginia Presidents!' he shouted, and off he ran to see them. I have seen two other Presidents, Jackson and John Quincy Adams. Adams was a fine little fellow. He had a solid look.

"After Mr. Jefferson returned from Washington, he was for years crowded with visitors, and they almost ate him out of house and home. They were there all times of the year; but about the middle of June the travel would commence from the lower part of the State to the Springs, and then there was a perfect throng of visitors. They travelled in their own carriages, and came in gangs—the whole family, with carriage and riding-horses and servants; sometimes three or four such gangs at a time. We had thirty-six stalls for horses, and only used about ten of them for the stock we kept there. Very often all of the rest were full, and I had to send horses off to another place. I have often sent a wagon-load of hay up to the stable, and the next morning there would not be enough left to make a hen's-nest. I have killed a fine beef, and it would all be eaten in a day or two. There was no tavern in all that country that had so much company. Mrs. Randolph, who always lived with Mr. Jefferson after his return from Washington, and kept house for him, was very often greatly perplexed to entertain them. I have known her many and many a time to have every bed in the house full, and she would send to my wife and borrow all her beds—she had six spare beds—to accommodate her visitors. I finally told the servant who had charge of the stable, to only give the visitors' horses half allowance. Somehow or other Mr. Jefferson heard of this; I never could tell how, unless it was through some of the visitors' servants. He countermanded my orders.

"One great reason why Mr. Jefferson built his house at Poplar Forest, in Bedford County, was that he might go there in the summer to get rid of entertaining so much company. He knew that it more than used up all his income from the plantation and every thing else, but he was so kind and polite that he received all his visitors with a smile, and made them welcome. They pretended to come out of respect and regard to him, but *I think* that the fact that they saved a tavern bill had a good deal to do with it, with a good many of them. I can assure you I got tired of seeing them come, and waiting on them. I knew just about as much about Mr. Jefferson's business as he did himself, and I knew that he could not stand it long. You know that he failed. This was after I left him, but I knew that it was bound to come. He had to pay $20,000 for Gov. Wilson C. Nicholas, whose daughter Jeff. Randolph married. I knew all about that matter. I went to see Gov. Nicholas a good many times on that business. Mr. Jefferson struggled on with that $20,000 several years, but that and his company finally broke him. After Gov. Nicholas broke, he came to live with Jeff. Randolph, and died there. I helped lay out his corpse, and had his grave dug.

"When the Governor died, he was very much in debt. People that he owed did not believe he was dead—they thought it was a trick to get rid of them. They came long distances, and would come to see me about it, and I had hard work to make them believe that he was dead and buried. While he was Governor, he once sent out an agent to meet the droves of hogs that were coming in to Richmond, and buy them up; and the butchers were compelled to buy them all of him. They were so mad that he had taken this way to make money out of them, that one night they covered the fence with hogs' entrails all around his house. After that they used to call him the 'Hog Governor.'

"When I left Mr. Jefferson, his grandson, Jeff.

$900 On or before the first day of October eighteen hundred and nineteen I promise to pay Edmund Bacon his heirs executors administrators or assigns the sum of nine hundred dollars with legal interest from the twelfth day of october 1818. to the true payment of which I bind myself my heirs executors and administrators. Witness my hand & seal this eighth (8) day of November 1818

Th. J. Randolph (seal)

ENDORSEMENT ON THE BACK.

Recieved from Thomas J Randolph the sum of five hundred and fourteen dollars in part of the within obligation

Sep 20 1819

E Bacon

LITH. OF SARONY, MAJOR & KNAPP. 449 BROADWAY, N.Y.

Randolph, took my place. He took charge of the business just as I had done for twenty years. I have loaned him money a great many times, and he has given me his note. Here is one of his notes, that is only part paid:

"'$900. On or before the first day of October, eighteen hundred and nineteen, I promise to pay Edmund Bacon, his heirs, executor, administrator, or assigns, the sum of nine hundred dollars, with legal interest from the twelfth day of October, 1818, to the true payment of which I bind myself, my heirs, executor, and administrator.

"'Witness my hand and seal, this eighth (8) day of November, 1818.

"'TH. J. RANDOLPH. [SEAL.]'

"This note is endorsed on the back as follows:

"'Received from Thomas J. Randolph the sum of five hundred and fourteen dollars, in part of the within obligation. E. BACON.

"'*Sept.* 20, 1819.'

[*See Facsimile.*]

"I knew Jeff. Randolph as well as one man can know another. Mr. Jefferson took great pains with his education, but he didn't take after his mother—he wasn't a Jefferson—he wasn't talented. He never wrote those letters* about Mr. Jefferson without help. I know him too well to believe that. He never saw the day that he could write those letters. I should like to see him again. I know we should take a good deal of pleasure talking over old times.

"I was very sorry to leave Mr. Jefferson; but I was more willing to do it, because I did not wish to see the poor old gentleman suffer, what I knew he must suffer, from the debts that were pressing upon him. I know that he thought a great deal of me. I had proofs enough of that, besides the letter I showed you. I know that if one man ever tried to serve another faithfully, I did him—and he was satisfied. One day he was at the blacksmith-shop, and * * * * * found some fault with me, and said my salary was too large. The blacksmith, who heard the conversation, told me of it, and said Mr. Jefferson replied, 'Not one man in a thousand would do as well for me as Mr. Bacon has done.'

"When we parted, it was a trying time to me. I don't know whether he shed any tears or not, but I know that I shed a good many. He was sitting in his room, on his sofa, where I had seen him so

---

* The letters published in *Randall's Life of Jefferson.* I carried this work to Capt. Bacon, and he read it with great interest during my visits.

often, and keeping hold of my hand some time, he said, 'Now let us hear from each other occasionally;' and as long as he lived I heard from him once or twice a year. The last letter I ever had from him was when I wrote him of the death of my wife, soon after I got to this country. He expressed a great deal of sympathy for me; said he did not wonder that I felt completely broken up, and was disposed to move back; that he had passed through the same himself; and only time and silence would relieve me. That is the letter I told you I so much regretted I had lost.

"I am now (1862) in my seventy-seventh year. I have seen a great many men in my day, but I have never seen the equal of Mr. Jefferson. He may have had the faults that he has been charged with, but if he had, I could never find it out. I don't believe that, from his arrival to maturity to the present time, the country has ever had another such a man."

CONCLUSION.

In the preparation of this volume, the author has preferred to confine his labors to a simple presentation of historical facts, leaving his readers to draw their own conclusions from the statements made. Whatever may be our individual views of Mr. Jefferson's public life, or his political or religious opinions, it surely is matter for pride and joy that one who knew him so long and well bears such testimony to his character.

While the author has been engaged in the preparation of this volume, lingering in spirit amid the sacred shades of Monticello, and dwelling upon its hallowed associations, an utterly causeless and wicked rebellion has culminated in the establishment of the so-called Confederate States.

The facts presented in this volume, while they increase our reverence for those master-builders who laid the foundations of our glorious Union, give intensity to our abhorrence of their traitorous successors, who are endeavoring to tear down the magnificent structure.

There could be no more sad and striking illustration of the folly and madness of this rebellion, than the fact that the home of Jefferson has been confiscated, because its owner is loyal to the Stars and Stripes. The banner of treason—the Confederate flag—now waves over the bones of the author of the Declaration of Independence. If this sad fact does not stir *them* in their resting-place, it surely will move every loyal heart to the rescue of that hallowed shrine. With all its historic associations, like Mount Vernon, it belongs to the entire nation. With God's blessing on our arms, in the future as in the past, we will associate Monticello with Quincy; Yorktown with Bunker Hill; Eutaw Springs with Saratoga; Marion's men in the swamps of the Santee with those at Valley Forge; and from these and all our old battle-fields we will gather flowers blushing with tints borrowed from the blood of their hallowed dead, with which to entwine wreaths and garlands for our rejoicings over our not distant and not inglorious peace.

And when that day comes,—as come it must, for we have only quicksands beneath our feet until we reach it,—when that day comes, and our dear old Ship of State is again moored in peaceful waters, shall we not love her as never before? Then she will have demonstrated not only to us, but to the nations of the earth, that she can sail in storm as well as calm; a storm such as Ship of State never weathered before, and in which a less gallant crew would inevitably have gone down.

Then, with new-born emphasis, we shall say:

"Sail on, O Ship of State!
Sail on, O Union strong and great!
Humanity, with all its fears,
With all the hopes of future years,
Is hanging breathless on thy fate!
We know what master laid thy keel,
What workmen wrought thy ribs of steel,
Who made each mast, and sail, and rope,
What anvils rang, what hammers beat,
In what a forge, and what a heat,
Were shaped the anchors of thy hope.
Fear not each sudden sound and shock;
'Tis of the wave, and not the rock;
'Tis but the flapping of the sail,
And not a rent made by the gale!
In spite of rock and tempest's roar,
In spite of false lights on the shore,
Sail on, nor fear to breast the sea,—
Our hearts, our hopes, are all with thee;
Our hearts, our hopes, our prayers, our tears,
Our faith triumphant o'er our fears,
Are all with thee! are all with thee!"

APPENDIX.

MR. JEFFERSON'S WILL.

"I, Thomas Jefferson, of Monticello, in Albemarle, being of sound mind, and in my ordinary state of health, make my last will and testament, in manner and form as follows:

"I give to my grandson, Francis Eppes, son of my dear deceased daughter, Mary Eppes, in fee simple, all that part of my lands at Poplar Forest, lying west of the following lines, to wit: beginning at Radford's upper corner, near the double branches of Bear Creek and the public road, and running thence in a straight line to the fork of my private road, near the barn; thence along that private road, (as it was changed in 1817,) to its crossing of the main branch of North Tomahawk Creek; and from that crossing in a direct line over the main ridge which divides the North and South Tomahawk, to the South Tomahawk, at the confluence of two branches where the old road to the Waterlick crossed it, and from that confluence up the northernmost branch, (which separates McDaniel's and Perry's fields,) to its source;

and thence by the shortest line to my western boundary. And having, in a former correspondence with my deceased son-in-law, John W. Eppes, contemplated laying off for him, with remainder to my grandson, Francis, a certain portion in the southern part of my lands in Bedford and Campbell, which I afterwards found to be generally more indifferent than I had supposed, and therefore determined to change its location for the better; now, to remove all doubt, if any could arise on a purpose merely voluntary and unexecuted, I hereby declare that what I have herein given to my said grandson Francis, is instead of, and not additional, to what I had formerly contemplated. I subject all my other property to the payment of my debts in the first place. Considering the insolvent state of the affairs of my friend and son-in-law, Thomas Mann Randolph, and that what will remain of my property will be the only resource against the want in which his family would otherwise be left, it must be his wish, as it is my duty, to guard that resource against all liability for his debts, engagements, or purposes whatsoever, and to preclude the rights, powers, and authorities over it, which might result to him by operation of law, and which might, independently of his will, bring it within the power of his creditors, I do hereby devise and bequeath all the residue of my property, real and personal, in possession or in action, whether held in my own right, or in that of my dear deceased wife, according to the powers vested in me by deed of settlement for that purpose, to my grandson, Thomas J. Randolph, and my friends, Nicholas P. Trist and Alexander Garret, and their heirs, during the life of my said son-in-law, Thomas

M. Randolph, to be held and administered by them, in trust, for the sole and separate use and behoof of my dear daughter, Martha Randolph, and her heirs; and, aware of the nice and difficult distinction of the law in these cases, I will further explain by saying, that I understand and intend the effect of these limitations to be, that the legal estate and actual occupation shall be vested in my said trustees, and held by them in base fee, determinable on the death of my said son-in-law, and the remainder during the same time be vested in my said daughter and her heirs, and of course disposable by her last will, and that at the death of my said son-in-law, the particular estate of the trustees shall be determined, and the remainder, in legal estate, possession, and use, become vested in my said daughter and her heirs, in absolute property forever. In consequence of the variety and indescribableness of the articles of property within the house of Monticello, and the difficulty of inventorying and appraising them separately and specifically, and its inutility, I dispense with having them inventoried and appraised; and it is my will that my executors be not held to give any security for the administration of my estate. I appoint my grandson, Thomas Jefferson Randolph, my sole executor, during his life, and after his death, I constitute executors, my friends, Nicholas P. Trist and Alexander Garret, joining to them my daughter, Martha Randolph, after the death of my said son-in-law, Thomas M. Randolph. Lastly, I revoke all former wills by me heretofore made; and in witness that this is my will, I have written the whole, with my own hand, on two pages, and have subscribed my name to each of them, this sixteenth day of March, one thousand eight hundred and twenty-six.

"TH. JEFFERSON.

"I, Thomas Jefferson, of Monticello, in Albemarle, make and add the following codicil to my will, controlling the same so far as its provisions go:

"I recommend to my daughter, Martha Randolph, the maintenance and care of my well-beloved sister, Anne Scott, and trust confidently that from affection to her, as well as for my sake, she will never let her want a comfort. I have made no specific provision for the comfortable maintenance of my son-in-law, Thomas M. Randolph, because of the difficulty and uncertainty of devising terms which shall vest any beneficial interest in him, which the law will not transfer to the benefit of his creditors, to the destitution of my daughter and her family, and disablement of her to supply him; whereas, property placed under the exclusive control of my daughter and her independent will, as if she were a *femme sole*, considering the relation in which she stands both to him and his children, will be a certain resource against want for all.

"I give to my friend, James Madison, of Montpellier, my gold-mounted walking-staff of animal horn, as a token of the cordial and affectionate friendship which for nearly now an half century has united us in the same principles and pursuits of what we have deemed for the greatest good of our country.

"I give to the University of Virginia my library, except such particular books only, and of the same edition, as it may already possess, when this legacy shall take effect; the rest of my said library, remaining after those given to the University shall have been taken out, I give to my two grandsons-in-law, Nicholas P. Trist and Joseph Coolidge. To my grandson, Thomas Jefferson Randolph, I give my silver watch in preference of the golden one, because of its superior excellence, my papers of business going of course to him, as my executor, all others of a literary or other character I give to him as of his own property.

"I give a gold watch to each of my grandchildren, who shall not have already received one from me, to be purchased and delivered by my executor to my grandsons at the age of twenty-one, and granddaughters at that of sixteen.

"I give to my good, affectionate, and faithful servant, Burwell, his freedom, and the sum of three hundred dollars, to buy necessaries to commence his trade of painter and glazier, or to use otherwise, as he pleases.

"I give also to my good servants, John Hemings and Joe Fosset, their freedom, at the end of one year after my death; and to each of them respectively, all the tools of their respective shops or callings; and it is my will that a comfortable log-house be built for each of the three servants so emancipated, on some part of my lands convenient to them with respect to the residence of their wives, and to Charlottesville, and the University, where they will be mostly employed, and reasonably convenient also to the interests of the proprietor of the lands, of which houses I give the use of one, with a curtilage of an acre to each, during his life, or personal occupation thereof.

"I give also to John Hemings the service of his two apprentices, Madison and Eston Hemings, until their respective ages of twenty-one years, at which period, respectively, I give them their freedom; and I humbly and earnestly request of the Legislature of Virginia a confirmation of the bequest of freedom to these servants, with permission to remain in this State, where their families and connections are, as an additional instance of the favor of which I have received so many other manifestations in the course of my life, and for which I now give them my last, solemn, and dutiful thanks.

"In testimony that this is a codicil to my will of yesterday's date, and that it is to modify so far the provisions of that will, I have written it all with my own hand in two pages, to each of which I subscribe my name, this seventeenth day of March, one thousand eight hundred and twenty-six.

"TH. JEFFERSON."

www.ingramcontent.com/pod-product-compliance
Lightning Source LLC
LaVergne TN
LVHW021406110826
845150LV00007B/1800

* 9 7 8 1 4 2 5 5 1 1 9 2 0 *